Series / Number 02-035

# Military Involvement
# in Politics:
# A Causal Model

**FRANK WHELON WAYMAN**
*University of Michigan*

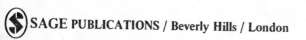

SAGE PUBLICATIONS / Beverly Hills / London

*For information address:*

SAGE PUBLICATIONS, INC.
275 South Beverly Drive
Beverly Hills, California 90212

SAGE PUBLICATIONS LTD
St George's House / 44 Hatton Garden
London EC1N 8ER

International Standard Book Number 0-8039-0525-4

Library of Congress Catalog Card No. 75-9033

FIRST PRINTING

When citing a professional paper, please use the proper form. Remember to cite the
correct Sage Professional Paper series title and include the paper number. One of the
two following formats can be adapted (depending on the style manual used):

(1) AZAR, E. E. (1972) "International Events Interaction Analysis." Sage Professional Papers in International Studies, 1, 02-001. Beverly Hills and London: Sage
Pubns.

*OR*

(2) Azar, Edward E. 1972. *International Events Interaction Analysis*. Sage Professional Papers in International Studies, vol. 1, series no. 02-001. Beverly Hills and
London: Sage Publications.

# CONTENTS

FRANK WHELON WAYMAN is engaged in further research on the political role of the military, as well as codirecting a four-wave panel study of voting behavior and partisan alignments, 1974-1976. He received his B.A. from Cornell University, his Ph.D. from the University of Pennsylvania, and is now Assistant Professor of Political Science at the University of Michigan, Dearborn.

# Military Involvement
# in Politics:
# A Causal Model

**FRANK WHELON WAYMAN**
*University of Michigan*

## INTRODUCTION

**Military involvement in politics** is the involvement of military officers in the making of national policy outside of the area of national defense. Students of military involvement are confronted with a host of insights provided by the major thinkers in the field, but understanding has been retarded in two key areas: (1) integrating the insights of these thinkers into a coherent theory, and (2) testing hypotheses in a rigorous, controlled fashion, so that the hypotheses might be ranked according to their actual importance. In this paper we have attempted to integrate the hypotheses and perspectives of the major thinkers into a coherent theory of decision-making, and to assess the relative importance of the various components of that theory through the technique of recursive causal modelling.

AUTHOR'S NOTE: *Several individuals have assisted in the preparation of this paper. My dissertation advisor, Willard Keim, and committee members, Charles Elder and Henry Wells, suggested improvements in the initial manuscript. Claude Welch, of the Political Science Department, SUNY-Buffalo, the staff of the Statistical Research Laboratory at the University of Michigan, as well as the anonymous reviewers for Sage Professional Papers were of assistance in the final stages. One Sage reviewer in particular suggested a number of key improvements. Don Anderson of the Political Science Department, University of Michigan, Dearborn, read the final draft and made stylistic revisions.*

A review of the literature yielded concepts and theories that have been used to explain military involvement in politics. These concepts and theories were reorganized and integrated into a formal model of rational choice. Several hypotheses were derived from this model. The variables in the hypotheses were operationalized. The 112 large nations that were independent from 1965 through 1968 were selected as the population for study, and data were successfully gathered for 110 of them. The model was shown to fit the data for all regions except Africa. Failure to disconfirm the model led to tentative acceptance of the theory.

In the formal model of choice, the key *values* are the legitimacy (L) a coalition attaches to civil as opposed to military rule, and the value (X) attached to holding formal political power and thereby excluding the other side. Also critical to the preference for military rule is the *likelihood* that military rather than civilian rule will succeed in keeping formal power in the coalition's hands. If these are the key parameters, and s is the probability that the coalition can set up a viable and effective military regime, and z is the probability that the coalition will hold power under civilian rule, it can be shown that it is rational to prefer military rule if $L < (s - z) X$. We label L, "legitimacy," X, "the intensity of cleavage," and (s − z), "the relevance of cleavage." We sharply contrast this balance between legitimacy and cleavages with Huntington's (1968) balance between institutionalization and social mobilization.

The model is used as a framework to relate a series of independent variables to the level of military involvement. These variables are integrated into a causal model, which is presented in Figure 1. Eight variables account for up to 66% of the variance in the level of military involvement. Variables ranked in terms of their total (direct plus indirect) effects are:

(1) the level of modernization,

(2) the level of institutionalization of the political party system,

(3) the degree of cleavage between the modern and traditional sectors,

(4) the nation's traditional form of civil-military relations,

(5) rapid urbanization in a context of discrimination and potential separatism,

(6) external wars,

(7) the total magnitude of civil violence, and

(8) central government expenditures as a percentage of gross domestic product.

Of the ideas of the major theorists on military involvement, Huntington's concept of political institutionalization proved the most important cause of military involvement. Second in importance were conflicts over modernization. Third in importance were the effects of external war, as suggested by Lasswell (1941). Fourth, some hypotheses of Andreski (1968) on the effects of civil discord on military involvement were weakly confirmed, but Andreski's emphasis on the importance of brute force, as measured by the military participation ratio, proved to have no measurable effect on the level of military involvement.

## ANALYSIS AND DEFINITION OF MILITARY RULE

The "military" is any hierarchically organized armed force which serves the state and which trains primarily to prepare for the exercise of controlled violence. Military involvement in politics, military rule, military regimes, military dictatorships, and similar terms refer to the same phenomenon throughout the text, although military involvement is a broad term that covers both full-blown military regimes and less complete military control of politics.

There is a defect both in ordinary language and in a large number of scholarly publications: "military intervention" (or involvement)—like "modernization," "integration," and a host of other concepts—often refers both to a state of affairs (military rule) and to the process leading to that state of affairs (a coup d'etat). In this paper, "military involvement," "military dictatorships," and "military regimes" will refer to the state of affairs—the *level* of military control. Coups and other events that increase the level of military control will be labelled "military intervention." In this paper, we will not attempt to explain military intervention.

Paradoxically, a cause of military intervention will not always be a cause of military rule. Consider the causes of revolutions in general. Amongst this set of variables, there may be some—such as economic recession or blatant government corruption—that trigger successful coups against civilian regimes (that is, *increases* in the level of military involvement), and also trigger revolutions that return rule to civilians (*decreases* in the level of military involvement). If the power of these causes of revolution is the same in both directions, then those variables that sometimes cause *increases* in the level of military intervention will not act, in the aggregate, as causes of military rule.

Studying military rule rather than military intervention simplifies measurement. If one is interested in military rule, one would measure the *level* of military involvement at time t relative to the level in other countries at that point in time. If one is interested in the process of becoming, one would have to measure the amount and direction of *change* in the level of military involvement from time t to time t+1 in country N relative to the amount and direction of change (a) in *other* countries from *any* t+i to t+i+1; or (b) in the *same* country from any t+i to t+i+1, i ≠ 0. This explains why most studies of military intervention have been national case studies. Since these studies lack the cross-national comparability which was specified above to be necessary in studying the *level* of military involvement, they have focused on the dynamic question of what causes *changes* in the level of military intervention. Usually, they have studied the causes of specific coups.

In using aggregate data over many countries, measurement problems are severe. Measuring change is especially difficult when measurement error is present, because the measurement error may be greater than the amount of change over time. For example, if the G.N.P. of a country is $100 million ± $10 million in 1950 and $105 million ± $10 million in 1960, it may have increased as much as 30% (from $90 million to $115 million) or decreased as much as 14% (from $110 million to $95 million). The error in the estimate of the level of G.N.P. was tolerable, but the possible error in

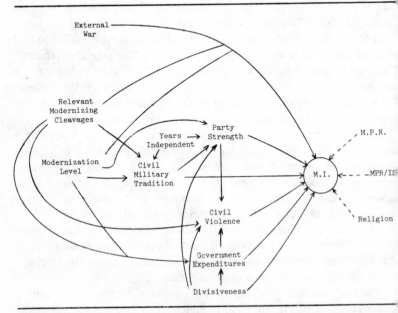

**FIGURE 1: Hypothesized Causal Model**

change of G.N.P. is enormous. This problem is more likely to arise if the data for the two points in time are not from the same source, for if they were from the same source one could assume a consistent bias in the measures.

Given the data available, it was judged best to work initially with predicting the level of military involvement to minimize the error. Hence, all quantitative work to date deals with the *level* of military involvement, rather than change in military involvement, as the dependent variable.

The level of military involvement will be measured by the form of military control. It is considered high if active military officers directly run the government, moderate if they govern from behind the scenes, and low if they do not govern at all. We do not argue that the form of military control is perfectly correlated with the intensity or scope of military control, or with the degree to which the government makes decisions in a military style. The intensity of military control is the degree of control the military has over government decisions in a certain issue area. The scope of military control is the number of issue areas over which the military exercises control. The military style of a regime is the processing of political decisions in a style normally characteristic of a military unit. Some possible relationships among these variables are that the indirect form of military rule involves the same intensity of control as direct military rule; that direct military rule is broader in the scope of military control than is indirect military rule; that direct military rule may make the use of the military decision making style more frequent than its use under indirect military rule.

Army officers—not naval officers, air force officers, or secret police officers—usually lead military government because of the strategy of a coup d'etat. First, the army operates on land, and land forces are generally critical to a coup because the objectives to be seized are specific buildings in the capital and other dominant cities. When, however, the capital is an ocean port and the country is dominated by the capital, the navy may play a political role, as in Argentina. Second, the army is usually by far the largest cohesive armed force in the country. Those staging a coup are usually a small, specialized body of troops (Metron, 1971), who intend a minimum of bloodshed. Hence they rely on the neutrality of most other troops in the country. This neutrality is usually assured if the troops staging the coup are army troops, since most other armed groups will feel a fraternal bond that prevents their marching against the rebels. With the army usually playing such a dominant role, virtually no regimes are run by police, navy, or air force. Where there is no army, as in Panama, the National Guard may occupy this traditional place of the army. Where a terroristic force is a better fighting force than the army, as in Haiti, it may supplant the army as the pillar of a military regime.

The operationalization of military involvement is to show an expert our definition of military involvement and ask him where he thinks the country lies on our scale of military involvement.

More objective measures of the degree of military influence are not available. One might count the number of military officers and former military officers in the cabinet. This measure, however, is insensitive to the cases in which the military is the power behind the throne. One might count the number of coups. The problems here are more severe: the measure is radically discontinuous, with, generally speaking, one coup one year followed by several years without a coup. How is one to infer the character of the years without a coup from the datum that a coup occurred one, two, or three years before? Frequent coups may indicate disagreement within the officers' corps rather than great military dominance; indeed, since this disagreement may concern whether or not the military should rule, frequent coups may signal a possible return to civilian rule.

The degree of military influence is based on two sources: the results of the Adelman-Morris (1967) questionnaire for 1957-1962, and the judgments of S. E. Finer (1971) for the period around 1969.

In the case of the Adelman-Morris scale, the authors produce eight levels of military involvement by combining a trichotomy (direct control by the military—indirect military rule—civilian rule) with data on the time span involved (direct control for the whole time span—for over half of the time span—for less than half of the time span—indirect control for the whole time span). Although Adelman and Morris did not rank all of the countries in our study, we were able to rank those they omitted without great difficulty because they are modern countries about which a great deal of data are available.

The eight categories are:

(A) Countries in which the military was in direct political control:

    (1) during the entire period 1957-1962

    (2) for most of the period 1957-1962

    (3) for one or two years 1957-1962

(B) Countries in which the military was an important political influence but was not in direct political control

(4) those in which the tie between the military and the civilian government was very close

(5) countries in (B) but not in (4) or (6).

(6) countries in which the ties between the military and the civilian government were significant for less than the entire period.

(C) Countries in which the military had little or no political influence

(7)

(8) degrees of category C

In the case of Finer's regime typology, we can get a large number of levels of military involvement by being willing to make fine discriminations about the level of military involvement at one point in time; Finer's data cover a one-year rather than a five-year interval, which makes consideration of the time span of military control impossible.

The categories based on Finer's analysis are designed to roughly parallel those of Adelman and Morris. Adelman and Morris used an eight point scale, and the analysis based on Finer uses a nine point scale. As in the case of the Adelman-Morris scale, the last two categories of the Finer-based scale (categories eight and nine) are reserved for the absence of military involvement. When this is clearly the case, the country gets a score of nine; when there is some doubt about the lack of military involvement, the country gets a score of eight.

As in the case of the Adelman-Morris scale, the first three points of the Finer-based scale (one, two and three) are reserved for direct military rule. Because Finer has several categories of direct military rule, the scale from one to three was broken into several subdivisions. First are the countries with clear-cut direct military rule. Sometimes these regimes are unadorned with any facade of civilian participation, but at other times they are adorned with some "fake or forced form of legitimation" such as a popular plebiscite or the establishment of a controlled assembly. These adornments Finer calls "quasi-civilianization," but they are just window dressing and do not affect the extent to which the regime is classified as a military regime. Within this first category of "direct military rule," Finer (1971: 576) differentiates regimes according to their degree of "subgroup" autonomy. The more the press, political parties, trade unions, industrial organizations, the clerisy, chiefs and shieks are able to play political roles independent of the directives of the military-led central government, the higher the "sub-group autonomy." To look at it the other

**TABLE 1**
**Military Involvement Scores**

| NATION | 1960 Adelman Morris | 1969 Finer | NATION | 1960 | 1969 |
|---|---|---|---|---|---|
| USA | 8 | 90 | Cameroun | 8 | 90 |
| Canada | 8 | 90 | Nigeria | 8 | 10 |
| Cuba | 5 | 90 | Gabon | 8 | 50 |
| Haiti | 2 | 10 | C. African R. | 8 | 10 |
| Dom. Rep. | 2 | 10 | Chad | 7 | 90 |
| Jamaica | 8 | 90 | Braz (Congo) | 8 | 10 |
| Trinidad | 8 | 90 | Kins (Congo) | 2 | 10 |
| Mexico | 8 | 90 | Uganda | 8 | 90 |
| Guatemala | 3 | 40 | Kenya | 6 | 90 |
| Honduras | 3 | 40 | Tanzania | 8 | 90 |
| El Salvador | 2 | 40 | Burundi | | 10 |
| Nicaragua | 2 | 40 | Rwanda | | 50 |
| Costa Rica | 8 | 90 | Somalia | 8 | 13 |
| Panama | 5 | 40 | Ethiopia | 4 | 50 |
| Colombia | 8 | 70 | Zambia | 8 | 90 |
| Venezuela | 4 | 70 | Malawi | 8 | 90 |
| Ecuador | 5 | 40 | S. Africa | 5 | 90 |
| Peru | 3 | 13 | Malg. | 8 | 90 |
| Brazil | 4 | 20 | Morocco | 8 | 60 |
| Bolivia | 8 | 13 | Algeria | 3 | 10 |
| Paraguay | 1 | 30 | Tunisia | 8 | 90 |
| Chile | 8 | 90 | Libya | 8 | 13 |
| Argentina | 3 | 13 | Sudan | 2 | 13 |
| Uruguay | 8 | 90 | Iran | 5 | 60 |
| U.K. | 8 | 90 | Turkey | 3 | 50 |
| Eire | 8 | 90 | Iraq | 4 | 13 |
| Neth. | 8 | 90 | UAR (Egypt) | 2 | 10 |
| Belgium | 8 | 90 | Syria | 2 | 13 |
| Luxembourg | 8 | 90 | Lebanon | 4 | 90 |
| France | 6 | 90 | Jordan | 4 | 50 |
| Switz. | 8 | 90 | Israel | 8 | 90 |
| Spain | 3 | 30 | Saudi Arabia | 8 | 90 |
| Portugal | 3 | 30 | Yemen | 3 | 40 |
| W. Germany | 8 | 90 | Afghanistan | 4 | 50 |
| Austria | 8 | 90 | C.P.R. | 8 | 80 |
| Italy | 8 | 90 | Taiwan | 5 | 30 |
| Albania | 8 | 90 | N. Korea | 8 | 90 |
| Yugoslavia | 8 | 90 | S. Korea | 3 | 30 |
| Greece | 8 | 10 | Japan | 8 | 90 |
| Cyprus | 8 | 90 | India | 8 | 90 |

TABLE 1 (Continued)

| NATION | 1960 Adelman Morris | 1969 Finer | NATION | 1960 | 1969 |
|---|---|---|---|---|---|
| U.S.S.R. | 8 | 90 | Pakistan | 2 | 17 |
| Finland | 8 | 90 | Burma | 2 | 10 |
| Sweden | 8 | 90 | Ceylon | 8 | 90 |
| Norway | 8 | 90 | Nepal | 5 | 60 |
| Denmark | 8 | 90 | Thailand | 2 | 17 |
| Mali | 8 | 15 | Cambodia | 5 | 60 |
| Senegal | 5 | 90 | Laos | 4 | 40 |
| Dahomey | 8 | 40 | N. Vietnam | 8 | 80 |
| Niger | 8 | 90 | S. Vietnam | 4 | 15 |
| Ivory Coast | 8 | 90 | Malaysia | 8 | 90 |
| Guinea | 8 | 90 | Philippines | 8 | 90 |
| Upper Volta | | 10 | Indonesia | 4 | 17 |
| Liberia | 8 | 90 | Australia | 8 | 90 |
| Sierra Leone | 8 | 50 | New Zealand | 8 | 90 |
| Ghana | 6 | 50 | | | |
| Togo | 8 | 10 | | | |

way, the more the political activities of these groups are controlled and directed by the military central government, the higher the sub-group dependency. Within Finer's category of direct military rule, we scored countries with high sub-group dependency 1.0, with moderate sub-group dependency 1.3, with low sub-group dependency 1.7. Those few countries not ranked by Finer on sub-group dependency are scored 1.5.

Finer's second category, "indirect/continuous" military rule, is really a form of direct rule, for the military gives all the orders and the civilian officials who are supposed to be ruling are ignored or over-ridden by the military if they refuse to follow the military's directives. Regimes of this sort were scored 2.0.

Third, what Finer (1971: 552) calls "military/dual" regimes are regimes in which "the military share power with organized civilian forces and the government of the day leans now on one support, now on the other." Often they are regimes, such as those of Franco in Spain, Chiang Kai-shek in Taiwan, and Park in South Korea, in which a military strong man made an effort to build up civilian support for himself through a political party or the allegiance of powerful interest groups. Such regimes receive a score of 3.0.

As in the case of the Adelman-Morris scale, we have three scale points for the middle range of countries (points four through six) in which the military allows civilians to rule but remains an important political influence. At 4.0 we have what Finer calls "indirect/intermittent" military rule. Although the civilians are allowed to decide most issues, intermittently the military will order them to do something, or will countermand civilian plans. These intermittent military orders are "often limited to a simple veto rather than a positive program" (Finer, 1971: 552). This category corresponds to Adelman-Morris' category (also scored 4.0) of regimes in which the times between the military and the civilian government were very close.

Countries that do not at the moment have even this degree of military involvement, but which have been plagued by frequent coups or have just recently completed a period of military rule, are coded 5.0 or 6.0. Scale position seven is reserved for a few countries which could not easily be assigned to the "no military influence" or "indirect military influence" categories.

There are obvious weaknesses in both the Adelman-Morris and the Finer-based scales of military involvement. For example, in the Adelman-Morris scale, the eight categories are logically improper in that category six cuts across category four. A country which had very close ties between the military and the government, but had them for less than the whole period, would fall in category 4 but also in category 6. We can only hope that the respondents, ignoring this methodological error, did their best to impressionistically rank order the countries in their region without strict attention to the Adelman-Morris categories.

The correlation coefficient between the Finer and Adelman-Morris scales is $r = .79$ for the 80 countries we will later study. This should not be interpreted as a reliability coefficient, since some of the disagreement is the result of measurement error, while some is the result of changes in the real level of military involvement in some of the countries over the 10 year interval between the two measurements.

If we used only one of the scales, we would be in danger of finding causal relationships that were the artifact of errors in that scale. By using both of them we have a check on that danger. Using a measure around 1960 and another around 1970 also helps reduce the danger that our findings might be drastically limited in temporal scope; if the coefficients are roughly similar for the two time periods, we have more general findings than if we measured the causal effects for only one of the time periods.

## REVIEW OF THE LITERATURE

Several authors have attempted to offer general explanations of military rule.[1] One model is Huntington's (1968) theory of the Praetorian Soldier. According to Huntington, military rule is one aspect of the disorder that results from an imbalance between the degree of social mobilization and the degree of political institutionalization. The more social mobilization—that is to say, the more groups entering the political arena—the stronger political institutions must be. This is a very pessimistic view of popular participation in politics. As the people become mobilized in politics, Huntington says, political institutions must be strengthened lest disorder result from mass behavior. Huntington's viewpoint seems to be that any expansion of political participation is a threat to "political order."

While in general agreement with Huntington's emphasis on the need for political institutionalization, we disagree herein with his treatment of social mobilization. It is more accurate to say that *political institutionalization must be commensurate with the salience of political cleavages* than with social mobilization per se. Such an emphasis on cleavages and conflict as causes of military involvement is more compatible with the writings of other theorists than is Huntington's emphasis on social mobilization.

Two schools of theorists who have devoted attention to the problems of military rule have concluded that social conflicts and cleavages are critical causes of military involvement. These conflict theorists present a second general model of military involvement. Unfortunately, while Huntington tended to dismiss the conflict side of the balance by emphasizing social mobilization, the conflict theorists have tended to ignore the institutionalization side of the balance, and have treated military rule as the inevitable outcome of social conflict—as if the political institutions were irrelevant to the outcome.

One scholar who emphasizes the importance of conflict and cleavages is Stanislav Andreski (1968: 125-26):

> Restraint on resort to violence can prevail only if certain conditions obtain. The first is that a society must be fairly homogeneous; sufficiently homogeneous for the beliefs regulating exercise and transmission of authority to be unequivocal and universally accepted.

A second, larger school of theorists who have emphasized the importance of these factors are Pye, Halpern (1963), Johnson (1962), Shils, and Nordlinger (1970). What all these authors have in common is an emphasis on military rule as an attempt to control the direction and pace of modernization, in a conflict situation in which different social groups and classes disagree in fundamental ways about the direction of their society. Some of these theorists have argued that the army is basically a modernizing force, while others have argued that the role of the army is basically conservative. Nordlinger attempts to unravel this paradox with the answer that the army will favor the middle class. This argument is introduced to account for the tendency of some armies to favor the status quo, while others favor development. Nordlinger, following Halpern and Huntington, argues that the military favor development until the middle class is well entrenched in power; the army then turns conservative to consolidate the position of the middle class. Whatever the answer to such debates, from our point of view the central fact is that all participants in the argument—proponents of the Modernizing Soldier thesis, proponents of the Anti-Modernizing Soldier thesis, and Nordlinger—are agreed that intense social conflicts are the cause of military intervention.

A third model of military rule is Harold Lasswell's (1941) model of the Garrison Soldier. The Garrison Soldier exploits any potential for foreign conflict in order to increase his power over the domestic political system. By emphasizing the external danger, the Garrison Soldier convinces the people that only he—the symbol and leader of national defense—is properly suited to lead the nation in crisis. The Garrison Soldier exhorts his nation to defend itself against foreign foes, and converts his nation into a fortress of fear which he governs through manipulation of these fears.

A fourth model of military rule is Huntington's theory of professionalism. The classic statement of this theory (Huntington, 1957) was succinctly laid to rest by Finer (1962), and was not resurrected in Huntington's next magnum opus (1968). Although considerable interest in the concept of professionalism still exists in the scholarly community, the difficulty of gathering aggregate data on the concept, as well as Finer's criticisms, led me to omit most of it from my model.

## THEORY

How can these disparate theories of military involvement be related to each other? The procedure followed is to analyze military involvement from the perspective of a rational decision maker who is trying to maximize the benefits accruing to his social group. This group is a coalition, composed of a military officers' clique, possibly in alliance with civilians.

We assume that he will prefer military to civilian rule depending on which maximizes his group's expected payoff in terms of two values. The two values that concern him are: the benefits or spoils his group derives from holding public office and excluding their enemies, and second, the value he ascribes to having a civilian rather than a military regime.

In pursuing these values, the decision maker must choose between military and civilian rule. The first possible choice is to work to establish or maintain a friendly military regime. If the decision maker chooses this course of action, the group may gain the value X, which they attach to holding power. They have a likelihood, s, of gaining these spoils under a military regime; s represents the probability that their military regime will be successful. Their expected payoff from choosing military rule is s times X.

On the other hand, civilian rule carries with it the value, L, that the group ascribes to civilian rule. There is also a probability, z, of holding power under civilian rule and thereby gaining the spoils of office (X). Thus, the expected value of civilian rule is zX plus L.

It is rational to prefer military rule (and act in accord with that preference) if the expected value of military rule, sX, is greater than the expected value of civilian rule, zX + L. In a democratic society, in which almost all are socialized to prefer democratic rule, virtually any sizeable group would tend to prefer the more open style and symbolism of a civilian regime to the rule of the military. L would therefore tend to be positive, and the group would therefore be inclined to prefer civilian rule. They would be dissuaded from that inclination if s, the probability of their holding public office under military rule, is greater than z, the probability of their holding office under civilian rule. Indeed, some simple algebraic manipulations yield the decision rule that it is rational to prefer military rule if $(s-z)X > L$; that is to say, if the value one attaches to holding office (X) times the likelihood $(s-z)$ of improving one's chances of holding office under military rule rather than civilian rule is greater than the value (L) one attaches to civilian rule. The product, $(s-z)X$, will be called the "salience of political cleavages." From the point of view of our model, the ideas of Huntington on Praetorianism and political institutionalization are really ways of emphasizing the need to build up L: the value of civilian political institutions. The views of the conflict theorists revolve around X and s–z, which we call the intensity and pragmatic relevance of political cleavages. The institutional side of the inequality was strongly emphasized by Huntington in his Praetorianism theory, but the other side of the inequality draws on the ideas of conflict and cleavage theorists (Andreski, Lieuwen) rather than on Huntington. Thus, the decision rule we have derived substitutes cleavage structures for the social mobilization emphasized by Huntington on the side of the balance which is a threat to civilian rule. While Huntington feared the unruliness of social mobilization, we emphasize the rational choice of groups in conflict with their enemies as the instigator of military rule. This change in conceptual focus will allow us to bring hypotheses based on Lieuwen and Andreski into our framework, whereas it was not clear how they fit into Huntington's framework. Shortly, we will also integrate the ideas of Lasswell into our framework, and will thereby have explained all the major writings on military involvement in terms of our general decision rule.

Much of the remainder of our analysis will focus on the social *conditions* under which the pragmatic relevance of cleavage, the intensity of cleavage, and the legitimacy of the civilian regime will take on values under which military involvement is likely.

Consider the tensions between our model and that of Riker (1962). Riker shows that under certain assumptions *all* coalitions will split the polity into two evenly divided groups, regardless of the uneven size of social groups. We have assumed that political coalitions will sometimes be of unequal size because of the unequal size of social groups.

Riker's model is made to fit n-person, zero-sum games with side payments where the players are rational and have perfect information. One critical difference between our model and Riker's is that in ours there are no side-payments. Individuals are locked into invariant groups, and groups are locked into invariant coalitions by this assumption. The dynamics of our model stem only from the fluctuations in group size which result from economic, demographic, and social change. What the lack of side-payments means in politics is that there are no payoffs for being on the winning side per se. Individuals and groups receive reward only when the government position on an issue is identical to their group's or coalition's position on the issue. "Winning" consists not of being in the majority, but of insuring that the majority is on your side of the issue; compromise is not possible with the opposite coalition, for you are willing to become a part of their winning coalition only at the price of their abandoning their side on the issue and coming over to your side, while they will join with you only if you give up your position. One result of this is that Riker's minimal winning coalition conclusion (size principle) is not valid in our system. For example, a winning coalition of three groups may have 90% support, while a losing coalition of one group has only 10% support.

Not all political cleavages are of this dichotomous sort in which compromise, and hence side-payments, are impossible. Several types of issues do have a dichotomous, either/or flavor, however. One type of issue is that made dichotomous because the participants in the conflict define the issues as principles on which compromise would be immoral. The process by which moral sentiments become attached to some issues remains unclear. Issues involving religious doctrine are of this moral sort, as are issues involving crime (a judge is either "permissive" or "good" when viewed by a rightist, "good" or a "responsive fascist" when viewed from the left).

A second kind of issue on which compromise is difficult is the kind in which the competing groups have clear boundaries between them and have designated each other as enemies. The nations of the world are often groups of this sort. Thus, in international politics the issues are often drawn in either/or terms. "Should we trade at all with Russia?" and "Should we have any public relations with China?" were dominant questions in American foreign policy during the Cold War; anyone who answered "yes" to them was in danger of being labeled a fifth columnist. He was thus discredited before he had a chance to qualify his remarks by saying which particular dealings with the enemy he thought were in our national interest. Too many people saw the issue as an either/or issue on which the middle ground of a mixed strategy was dangerous.

A third type of either/or issue, discussed by Schelling (1960), is the set of issues which people see as qualitative rather than quantitative. On these issues, political activists can see only two "natural" or tenable positions. Thus, for example, in international politics the Soviet Union and the United States must compromise on the use of nuclear weapons or risk destroying each other. The compromise might be "use only one nuclear weapon a year, and never use it against the other power." But instead the compromise has been "never use nuclear weapons." The same has been true of gas warfare, on which a humane compromise might have been "use only gas that does no permanent damage." Instead, the rule has been "use no gas." Schelling suggests that these absolute rules have been adopted not simply because of the moral element (which does not often dominate decisions in international affairs) but also because there is one and only one clearcut leap involved—from using none to using the first amount. Violators who jump into making the first gas attack or using the bomb are easy to spot and censure; but a jump from, say, gas that incapacitates for a day to gas that incapacitates for a week is not clear cut, and this opens the way for creeping escalation without end.

In order for our analysis to be valid, some of the issues dividing the groups must be dichotomous because the groups involved perceive each other as enemies, because the issues are seen as matters of principle, or because the political actors see only two tenable positions on the issue.

# IMPLICATIONS OF THE THEORY

In a loose way, several hypotheses can be linked to this analytical framework. The hypotheses presented below will be, first, those dealing with conflict and cleavage, and, second, those dealing with the legitimacy of civilian rule and the strength of civilian political institutions.

## Cleavages and Military Rule

**Hypothesis 1**: *The higher the level of modernization and social mobilization, the lower the level of military involvement.*

Modernization will reduce the likelihood of military involvement because the concomitant political mobilization and social differentiation create an environment in which it is increasingly difficult to repress political activity by primary reliance on force. In relatively modernized societies, force and command become increasingly inappropriate vehicles for eliciting compliance. Rapid social and economic differentiation occur with modernization, and to an increasing extent effective running of the society requires the cooperation of many diverse groups. Since such groups are necessary to maintain the society free of major breakdown, they cannot simply be ordered to "comply or be shot," for they know they are needed to run the society smoothly. In such relatively modernized societies, oligarchic control over social groups can only be secured by massive external intervention (for example, the Soviet Union in Hungary and Czechoslovakia) or by a gradually moderating oligarchy with full control of the institutionalized socialization and communications media, such as the C.P.S.U. (for Russia, see Fleron, 1969). The military is not likely to have the skills necessary for such internal control.

To sum up, because of their lack of appropriate skills and because of the increasing ineffectiveness of force and command as instruments of power, the military is not likely to be able to effectively govern a relatively modernized society, and hence military involvement in such relatively modernized societies is likely to be low and limited at most to "veto coups," in which the military intervenes just long enough to replace one group of civilians with another. In terms of our model, modernization reduces the likelihood(s) of successful military rule, and thereby reduces the relevance of cleavages (s–z).

Nonetheless, some highly modernized societies have military governments. At the time of this study, Spain and Argentina were the most modern societies characterized by military involvement in politics. What can account for anomalies such as the authoritarian nature of government in these two relatively advanced societies? Continuing on our assumption that a politically mobilized populace will put a damper on military involvement in politics, *if very few people are active or concerned about politics, military dominance will be an easy matter.* Indeed, under these conditions, the military may be so politically dominant as to be able to intervene primarily on their own initiative, even without any allies among civilian social groups. For example, the military may intervene because an officer faction sees a chance to get rich by running the government. As Kling (1956) puts it, in such cases, "government does not merely constitute the stakes of a struggle among rival economic interests; government itself is a unique base of economic power." This assumes a very low level of political institutionalization, such that the populace will tolerate the running of the government as a purely private praetorian bailiwick for the praetorian's own profit; this state of affairs exists today in only a few states, such as perhaps Paraguay, Nicaragua, and Haiti in Latin America.

Such public indifference to the raiding of public coffers seems most likely in states where the public coffers are very small, and where the government does not affect most people's lives through heavy taxation or the provision of important social services.

**Hypothesis 2:** *Low governmental expenditures as a percentage of gross domestic product will make praetorian military involvement likely.*

In the light of these arguments, one should note that in Gurr's (1969) ranking of the central government expenditures of 117 nations as a percentage of gross domestic product, Spain and Argentina—which share the anomaly of being the most modern countries under military rule—rank 116th and 97th respectively. The aforementioned Haiti, Paraguay, and Nicaragua rank 113th, 109th, and 106th respectively.

**Hypothesis 3:** *A high percentage of a nation's manpower in the armed forces will lead to a high level of military involvement.*

Another variable which may affect the success of military involvement is the military strength of the armed forces relative to the other potential and actual armed groups in the society, such as police, militia, and guerrillas. Andreski, who coined the term "military participation ratio" (M.P.R.), has argued (1968: 124) that the greater the number of soldiers relative to civilians, the greater the likelihood of military regimes.

There are at least two ways in which one might measure this military strength of the armed forces. On the one hand, it may be simply the percentage of population in the military that matters:

**Hypothesis 3a:** *The higher the military participation ratio, the greater the level of military involvement.*

On the other hand, we might want to assume that the fractionalization of armed groups is a better measure of the potential that any one armed group has of dominating the military scene. If one armed force, such as the army, is much larger than the next larger armed force, such as the militia, then the larger armed force may be in a better position to dominate the country militarily and politically than if the two forces were more equal in size. An enormous preponderance of men in the army as compared to men in the militia may, therefore, increase the likelihood of successful military involvement. In that case, we would say:

**Hypothesis 3b:** *The higher the ratio of the largest armed force to other armed forces' strength, the greater the level of military involvement.*

Some scholars, however, have emphasized that coups involve only a few troops and little or no bloodshed. Recently, coups have been staged in Africa by miniscule armies. Other coups have been staged by even more miniscule groups within armies. In Sierra Leone, a group of warrant officers staged a successful coup by imprisoning almost all army and police officers and returning the country to civilian rule (Welch, 1970: 293). In Latin America, Anderson argues (1967: ch. 4), coups are not so much the exercise of brute force as the demonstration that the old regime no longer holds the loyalty of the army. Hence, rather than massive troop movements, only a few troops are needed to seize "high visibility" installations like the radio transmitter and the presidential palace, thereby producing a successful coup. In the light of these insights into the political process, it might not be surprising to find that brute force, as measured by military participation ratios, has little or no effect on the level of military involvement.

**Hypothesis 4:** *Conflicts during the transition to modernity will increase the level of military involvement.*

Many impressionistic observers have perceived an incorrect relationship between development and military involvement and they have argued that the more developed the country, the lower the level of military involvement. Halpern (1963) has come closer to the truth when he argued that, at least in its early stages, development does not decrease military involvement. Lieuwen (1960) anticipated the correct relationship when he argued that modernization and the emergence of modern sectors has initially caused the level of military involvement to increase.

In Latin America, according to Lieuwen, social conflicts between old social groups and the new groups created by modernization (Halpern's new middle class) caused a relapse into military intervention. Lieuwen differs

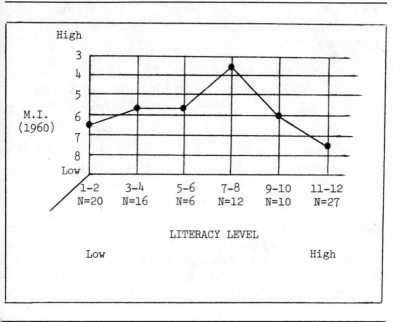

**GRAPH 1: Military Involvement as a Function of Percent of Population Literate.**
SOURCE: Adelman and Morris (1967) and supplementary sources cited herein.

from Halpern only in refusing to assert that in his region the military is always on the same side. Graph I supports Lieuwen's argument.

In terms of our model, military rule is occurring in these transitional societies because the relevance (s−z) of modernizing cleavages has increased. That is, several crucial sets of issues concerning modernization have reached a point where the advocates of each position are so equally balanced that political strategy may be decisive in affecting the outcome. The critical political strategy in our decision-making model is the choice between military and civilian rule. When that choice can make a difference, s−z can take on a positive value. This positive value may be high enough to overcome L, the generally high degree of legitimacy of civilian government.

When group A (say, a group of radical modernizers) is miniscule, s and z are both near zero for it. As group A's supporters grow towards 100% of the society, s and z approach one. Only when the group is at an intermediate size can cleavage relevance (s−z) become a large positive number.

Then, as a first possibility, the out-group may conspire with a military faction to stage a coup. This will occur when the out-group is impatient and wants success now. The out-group may have little affection for the current regime because of the manipulation of the four barriers—legitimation, incorporation, representation, and majority power (Lipset and Rokkan, 1967)—excluding the out-group from participation.

This bid for power by the out-group may have an analog in international relations. Organski (1958) has suggested that when two coalitions in the balance of power are approaching parity in power capabilities:

(1) war becomes likely,

(2) the weaker coalition (the analog of our out-group) will start the war, and

(3) it will attack prematurely and lose.

Organski's third proposition is not as interesting in the case of domestic politics, because of the high probability of several rematches between the two sides. That is, even if the proposition is valid for the first coup, the domestic out-group cannot be wiped out and in a few years may be even stronger and wiser and be able to make a successful coup.

The second possibility is that the in-group may, as the out-group grows in size, put its hopes in a coup as the means of erecting an impassable fourth barrier to the dangers of a majority out-group. The in-group may therefore conspire with its supporters in the military and stage a coup to set up a military regime.

The third possibility is that the military—fearful of being divided by such bids from both sides—may seize power and attempt to end the period of high political salience, either by resolving the divisive issues one way or another or by declaring a moratorium on the issues.

In any case these strategies will often entail a prolonged period of military involvement—in order to keep the conflict suppressed in the last case (possibility three), or in order to see to it that their decision on it is implemented and is accepted as final in the others.

**Hypothesis 5**: *When a high rate of social mobilization occurs in a context of intense political cleavage, the level of military involvement will increase.*

Heretofore, our model has treated social mobilization in the opposite way from Huntington. We have argued that a high *level* of social mobilization will reduce the level of military involvement. However, we would now argue (compare Deutsch, 1961) that *in the context of intense cleavage* a high *rate* of social mobilization will increase the level of military involvement. We will test our argument by seeing if rapid urbanization in a context of high discrimination and potential separatism causes a high level of military involvement. We will refer to the product of urbanization and discrimination and potential-separatism as "divisiveness."

In terms of our model, rapid social change increases the uncertainty with which the ruling elite views the future, and this uncertainty decreases the potential success of civilian rule (z). When there is no change, one expects one's group to remain at its current size and influence. The in-group's control over the status quo is not threatened. When there is rapid social change, producing complete uncertainty, the probability that the out-group will hold power under an open, civilian regime increases to 0.5. This threat to the in-group might be reduced to zero if the in-group could set up a military regime that forcefully and permanently excluded the other side from power. If so, $S-Z = 1.0-0.5$: the pragmatic relevance of M.I. is positive. The in-group has reason to support an existing friendly military regime, or stage a coup to establish one if it does not yet exist. So rapid social change, and the threat it poses of transfers of power in the relatively vulnerable and open civilian political system, tempt the in-group to resort to military rule.

If the out-group anticipates such efforts to shut them out of power, they may attempt a pre-emptive coup and establish a military regime of their own.

Our assumption of rationality may understate the importance of uncertainty as a cause of military involvement. One could argue that under conditions of increased uncertainty, when people have an opportunity of taking decisive action (such as a coup), people tend to "fear the worst"; more precisely, they tend to "irrationally" assign a higher subjective probability to things getting worse under the current system than is warranted by uncertainty alone. Thus, in the example of complete uncertainty, the subjective evaluation of probability, $(s-z)_s$, is greater than the maximum rational probability estimate, $s-z = 0.5$.

Of course, the intense cleavages are themselves causes of military involvement, even when rapid social mobilization is not occurring.

**Hypothesis 5a**: *High discrimination and potential separatism lead to high levels of military involvement.*

Actually, certain types of rapid social mobilization may create intense social cleavages which then interact with the social mobilization to create a high level of military involvement. Rapid urbanization, for example:

(1) creates major new groups (labor, middle class, industrialists) whose novelty in the political arena creates uncertainty as to their political behavior once in power,

(2) brings these groups together in a setting where

    (a) conflicts between them are not mitigated by the cohesive forces of a small community, and where

    (b) bad consequences (such as unemployment) of these conflicts are not softened by the protection of community and extended family,[2] and

(3) creates in these new groups a modern culture antithetical to the traditional culture, so that there exists at the same time two nations.

Hence, rapid urbanization is rapid change in a setting of intense cleavage, and one might indeed argue that rapid urbanization increases both the pragmatic relevance of cleavage (by increasing the probability that power will change hands) and the intensity of cleavages (by making it unclear what the rapidly emerging and changing other side stands for, so that one tends to fear the worst). Hence:

**Hypothesis 5b**: *Rapid urbanization increases the level of military involvement.*

## War and Military Rule

**Hypothesis 6**: *War will increase the level of military involvement.*

**Hypothesis 7**: *Revolution will increase the level of military involvement.*

When troops are needed to actively defend the regime, the importance of the military is enhanced. The loyal population sees the military as performing a vital function of government—protecting the nation from external attack or internal subversion. The military see themselves suddenly as very important members of the state apparatus. At the same time, by distinguishing themselves on the field of battle, military heroes may emerge with broad popular support (both within the military and among civilians). For these reasons the civilian regime must be deferential to its military hierarchy.

Meanwhile, as defensive military actions increase in magnitude—and as military effort becomes more critical to regime survival—more and more spheres of social life are perceived as critical to the war effort, and hence as deserving close scrutiny and regulation by defense boards composed mostly of military men, whose supposed expertise and known concern not only win them seats on the boards but also make the civilians deferential to military wishes. In this way the civilian regime gradually yields decision-making power to the military. This yielding may not be sufficient because of the inertia of civilian leaders who wish to hold onto their accustomed power. Then the military may violently seize power, either when the war is being won because of their enhanced sense of competence, or when the war is being lost in order to remove the civilian-imposed restrictions which the army may blame for its losses. Thus, either through civilian deference or military coup, the military will become extremely influential in politics in such circumstances.

Further, if in domestic violence the government calls on the troops to fire on civilians, this may provoke immediate military involvement (Finer, 1962: 27):

> The professional army often vents its discomfort at having to act against its own nationals by blaming the "politicians," and by thinking of itself as being "used" by them for their own sordid purposes. The strain ... often impels them ... to act against the government.

Given the deep antagonisms between civilian coalitions in such violent times, the conditions will frequently be ideal for the military intervention to lead to a long period of military rule.

Revolutions, or "internal wars," increase the likelihood of military involvement by increasing the cleavages within society and by decreasing the legitimacy of civilian governments. External wars increase military involvement by increasing the legitimacy of military rule. We will now look at some other variables associated with the legitimacy and institutionalization of political institutions.

## Legitimacy, Institutionalization, and Military Rule

**Hypothesis 8**: *Strong political party systems will reduce the level of military involvement.*

What particular civilian political institutions are most important as bulwarks against military rule? Surely, political parties would be included on anyone's list. Except perhaps in a city-state or something smaller, democracy requires an organized link between the people and policy outcomes, and political parties provide that link.

> The political party emerges whenever the activities of a political system reach a certain degree of complexity, or whenever the notion of political power comes to include the idea that the mass public must participate or be controlled. ... The political party materialized when the tasks of recruiting political leadership and making public policy could no longer be handled by a small coterie of men

unconcerned with public sentiments. The emergence of a political party clearly implies that the masses must be taken into account by the political elite [La Palombara and Weiner, 1966: 3-4].

Because of the central role of the political party in channeling participation, Huntington (1968: 398) makes political parties the core of his explanation of military rule:

> The future stability of a society with a low level of political particiption thus depends in large part on the nature of the political institutions with which it confronts modernization and the expansion of political participation. The principal institutional means for organizing the expansion of political participation are political parties and the party system.

**Hypothesis 9**: *Catholic and Moslem countries should have a high level of military involvement because of their political culture.*

Catholic and Moslem countries have a high incidence of military rule, and innumerable scholars have argued that this can be explained by the "authoritarian" character of these two religions. Our data show that Moslem and Catholic countries do have a higher incidence of military rule than other countries. The critical question is whether factors other than religion can account for this (Przeworski and Teune, 1970). The causal models are designed to shed light on such questions.

**Hypothesis 10**: *A historical tradition of military rule will increase the level of military involvement.*

Historical factors are frequently alleged to be partially responsible for military involvement in politics. There are at least three aspects to such an allegation. The first possibility is that the independent causes of military involvement, such as civil violence or social differentiation, may have a time-lag effect. This possibility may be statistically tested by gathering data on both the independent and dependent variables over more than one point of time.

The second possibility is that an independent variable may be correlated with itself across time. Thus, military involvement may be slow to change merely because of the sluggishness of change in the independent variables.

The third possible cause of historical continuity is that the dependent variable may be self-perpetuating (negative feedback at work): once military involvement has occurred in a polity, its persistence is therefore likely, other things being equal.

Much of the evidence for such self-perpetuation of military involvement is simply that coups seem to be endemic in certain areas of the world, such as Latin America and the Middle East. Such evidence is faulty, however, insofar as such perpetuation may merely be the result of perpetuation of the independent variables and/or time-lag causation, rather than a case of true negative feedback. Thus, for example, one could argue that the persistence of coups in the Middle East and Latin America is a consequence of the authoritarianism of these areas, which stems from their continued adherence to Islam and Catholicism.

The statistical way to resolve this dilemma is to first attempt to explain all possible variance by utilizing all relevant time-lagged independent variables, and then introducing past military involvement levels to see if they explain anything further. For example, Putnam (1967: 104-05) found a 0.71 correlation ($r^2 = 0.50$) between Latin American coups in 1951-1955 and in 1961-1965. This may be the result of persistent independent variable causation, or it may be the result of self-perpetuation of the dependent variable, or both. If we utilize all relevant independent variables in a test and achieve an $R^2$ of 0.60, and *then* introduce this historic past of military involvement and achieve an $R^2$ of 0.80, then we are on relatively safe ground in arguing that 20% (0.80 − 0.60) of the variance can be accounted for by historic memory (negative feedback). At least some of the persistence of the sort Putnam found is the result of negative feedback. Through more detailed examination of the cases, the 20% could then be broken down into that resulting from simple regime perpetuation—those countries experiencing no significant political change over the period—and that resulting from the genuine continuation of a tradition running from one military dictatorship to another.

It will be necessary to control for the following effect in our statistical analysis.

**Hypothesis 11:** *Nations that have just become independent are highly unlikely to have military regimes.*

This is because power is initially transferred to a civilian government. Graph 2 illustrates this relationship for Africa. Only one of the countries listed as having a successful coup in the first nine years reverted to civilian rule in that time, so there was a steady increase in the number of countries with military regimes.

These hypotheses do not exhaust the list of proposed causes of military involvement. They do seem to represent a large portion of the dominant themes in the literature. They are the hypotheses that will be considered in our models.

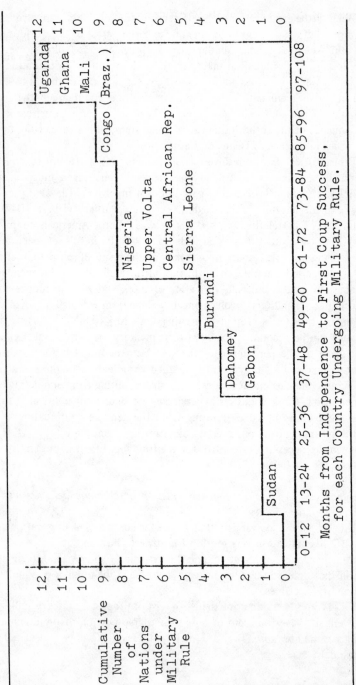

GRAPH 2: Growth of Military Involvement in Africa During the First Decade of Independence.

## Summary of Direct Causes of Military Rule

This completes our analysis of the direct causes of military involvement. The argument is summarized in Table 2. In this table, the causal effect of any variable is logically implied—if our arguments have been correct—by the causal effect of any variable to its left.

To summarize our argument, military involvement can occur under some circumstances without the collusion of civilian groups, but in most contemporary cases military involvement reaches its greatest possible extent when the military can exploit cleavages in the civilian populace. In a few very *backward societies,* military regimes may be still possible regardless of the cleavage structure, for only a small number of civilians will be politically conscious and in a position to thwart military ambitions. Here the low level of modernization and government activity preserves the possibility of the type of military involvement cited by Kling. In countries involved in *external war,* the level of military involvement will rise regardless of the cleavage structure. Here the civilians are more numerous and powerful, but defer to the military because of the existence of a military crisis.

In countries where civilian mobilization is widespread (and which are not engaged in external war), military involvement will be possible only when the *legitimacy* (L) of the civilian regime is low, and when *salient* (X(s−z)) political *cleavages* make it possible for the military to gain the cooperation of one of the mobilized civilian coalitions.

We have presented hypotheses relating each of these concepts to military involvement.

We have eleven testable hypotheses in the right hand column of Table I. These will allow us to test the validity of the theoretical structure. If any of the eleven testable hypotheses is found to be false, we will be forced to conclude that a portion of the theoretical structure is invalid.

If *all* the hypotheses related to one theoretical factor (say, L) are false, we would have to consider that portion of the theory invalid, but the rest of the theory would remain intact.

If only *some* of the testable hypotheses related to some theoretical factor were false, the factor might still be considered valid.

Finally, if *none* of the testable hypotheses are false, the theory will have received some support because it has weathered the storm of an empirical test. But all this evidence does not *prove* the theory, for other theories might conceivably imply the same set of testable hypotheses; thus the hypotheses might be true because of the workings of some alternative theory. To argue that the theory is proven by the confirmation of its

**TABLE 2**
**Summary of Hypotheses**

| CONCEPT | DERIVED HYPOTHESES |
|---------|--------------------|
| S | H.1: level of modernization |
| | H.2: low governmental expenditures |
| | H.3a: MPR |
| | H.3b: MPR/ISF |
| S-Z | H.4: relevant modernizing cleavages |
| Z | H.5b: urbanization rate |
| X | H.5a: discrimination and potential separatism |
| | H.7: civil violence |
| X(S-Z) | H.5: urbanization rate times discrimination and separatism |
| L | H.7: civil violence |
| | H.6: external wars |
| | H.8: political parties' strength |
| | H.9: religious authoritarianism |
| | H.10: previous military rule |
| CONTROL | H.11: recent independence |

testable hypotheses is to commit the logical error of affirming the consequent. This means that a theory can be disproved, by finding that there is no evidence for it, but can never be proven. At best, it can be shown that the theory does at the moment square with the available evidence.

## Indirect Causes of Military Rule

Two types of indirect effects must be specified in doing a causal analysis. It is necessary to specify:

(a) which of the causal variables listed in the right hand column of Table I has an indirect effect on military involvement through another of the causal variables in Table I, and

(b) whether there are any other variables (exogenous variables) that have an effect on more than one of the causal variables in the right hand column of Table I.

Until now we have specified only direct effects on military involvement. Each testable direct effect was derived from the four causal factors (S, Z, X, L) and their interactions. In listing our hypotheses about indirect effects, we will not be guided by such a theoretical scheme, but will rather state hypotheses because they have been suggested by authorities on the concepts in question or because there is considerable evidence for them.

**Hypothesis 12**: *Modernization strengthens political party systems.*

**Hypothesis 13**: *Divisiveness weakens political party systems.*

This hypothesis (13) is particularly relevant because it involves an interaction between divisiveness $(x(s-z))$ and legitimacy (L). As $s-z$ or X increases, not only do the payoffs $(x(s-z))$ of possible military involvement increase, but the costs (L) decline as well. As politics comes increasingly to be perceived as dominated by the salient, divisive struggle between the two rival coalitions, the political institutions are increasingly perceived to be mere tools in the hands of one faction or the other. This alienates the excluded faction from the political institutions. It also disgusts any by-standers who are not polarized by the cleavage in question; they too become alienated from the political structures. Lieuwen (1964: 112) amongst others, has referred to this indirect effect of political cleavages:

The military [when it intervenes] also has its civilian apologists—in the business community, in the professions, and among the landholders. Such men have generally become discouraged with all civilian political parties, both their leaders and their followers. They believe that an enforced order is essential to progress and that without military intervention disorder and chaos would prevail. They consider civilian parties incapable of running their countries and feel that their constant feuding and fractioning leads only to stalemate and drift. Consequently, the military has to occupy the power vacuum created, or else the nation will simply disintegrate.

**Hypothesis 14**: *The longer since independence, the greater the party system strength.*

This relationship must be specified because years since independence will also affect the military tradition score, which is a function of the number of coups. Whenever two endogenous variables are caused by a third variable, the two causal links must be specified and the causal paths used as partials in the regressions (Heise, 1969).

**Hypothesis 15**: *With a time lag, military involvement probably weakens party system strength.*

The statement of this hypothesis is crucial to our causal model. If military involvement does cause the weakening of political parties, as well as weak party strength causing military involvement, then we have a non-recursive model; and a non-recursive model will cause an intercorrelation of error terms that we have had to assume does not exist in order to use recursive estimation techniques.

Huntington (1968: 409), who has made the most detailed study of the relationship between military involvement and political institutionalization, asserts that the relationship is non-reciprocal:

Military coups do not destroy parties; they ratify the deterioration which has already occurred.

He proceeds to give a number of examples to support his assertion. Nevertheless, it did seem likely that after a prolonged period of military rule, parties would begin to atrophy from being unable to perform their functions of providing direct access to the political elite. Therefore, we hypothesized that after a number of years of military rule, parties would begin to weaken.

By stating this causal relationship as a time lag relationship, it is possible to continue to use ordinary least squares (recursive) estimation, by assuming that military involvement at time $t_2$ or $t_3$; and by assuming that error terms for military involvement at $t_1$ and at $t_2$ are uncorrelated

**Hypothesis 16**: *No other variable in the final causal model causes party institutionalization.*

**Hypothesis 17**: *The level of modernization affects the nation's military involvement tradition.*

Modern nations will have long ago passed through the stage of military involvement.

**Hypothesis 18**: *The relevance of developmental conflicts will affect the level of traditional military involvement. The more relevant the divisions, the more the military will intervene.*

**Hypothesis 19**: *The longer the period of independence, the greater the opportunity for a military involvement tradition to have developed.*

**Hypothesis 20**: *Since the other variables which cause military involvement are measured at time $t_1$, they cannot cause the military involvement tradition, since it is defined as military involvement at time $t_0$.*

This part of the specification problem is straightforward. Civil-military tradition is a variable operationalized to cover the period 1900-1956. "External wars" covered the period 1946-1968, heavy weighting given to the period since 1957. All other variables in the causal model (party system strength, total magnitude of civil violence, divisiveness, and central government expenditures) are measured during the period 1955-1963. Since causation does not operate backwards through time, these variables measured at time $t_1$ cannot cause the civil-military tradition at time $t_0$.

**Hypothesis 21**: *Divisiveness increases the total magnitude of civil violence.*

**Hypothesis 22**: *Central government expenditures decrease the total magnitude of civil violence.*

This hypothesis was confirmed by Gurr (1969), when using the same data.

**Hypothesis 23**: *Party system strength decreases the total magnitude of civil violence.*

**Hypothesis 24**: *Relevance of modernizing cleavages increases the total magnitude of civil violence.*

**Hypothesis 25**: *Modernization decreases the total magnitude of civil violence.*

**Hypothesis 26**: *None of the other causal variables in the final model affects the total magnitude of civil violence.*

The final four of these hypotheses concerning indirect effects are related to central government expenditures. In our most parsimonious model, they will by dropped, with a loss of only 2% in explained variance and great increase in parsimony. Although the statistics indicate that these hypotheses are valid, omitting these complicated effects involving central government expenditures will not greatly change the predictions of the model.

**Hypothesis 27**: *The more modern, the higher the central government expenditures as a percent of the GNP.*

Since relevant modernizing cleavages divide a society and thus make its central government less effective,

**Hypothesis 28**: *Societies with high developmental cleavages should tend to have lower central government expenditures than one would otherwise expect.*

For the same reasons,

**Hypothesis 29**: *Divisiveness should lower central government expenditures.*

**Hypothesis 30**: *No other variables in the model affect central government expenditures.*

The path diagram (Figure 1) not only summarizes out hypotheses, but also allows us to see how each of the major theories of military involvement fits into the overall model. We will now spell out in more detail how these theories are related to our model. In his review of the literature, Perlmutter (1970) has pointed out the limited perspective of even the major theorists:

> Going over the literature [on military involvement] and especially the contributions of the influential authors mentioned earlier, we find strong ties between their conceptual and analytical positions and the political and ideological climate of the times . . . . [Of the] four different analytical models . . . ., all [are] closely related to the politico-ideological weltanschauung of the authors.

Given this limitation of perspective, it should not be surprising that the major thrust of each theorist's ideas should encompass only a portion of our general model.

Let us consider first Andreski. In discussing Andreski, we must point out that many of his concepts, and especially his concept of social "homogeneity," are too vague for precise comparison with the variables in our model.

A portion of our model shows that relative deprivation, divisiveness, and relevance of cleavages all cause violence, and violence in turn causes military involvement. This portion of the model is an intellectual descendant of Andreski's argument that "heterogeneity" and poverty cause violence, which in turn causes military involvement.

Andreski's proposition that the size of the army affects the level of military involvement has, of course, been included in our model through the hypotheses on M.P.R. and MPR/ISF.

Lasswell's Garrison State model is embraced by our hypothesis on the effects of external war.

The Modernizing Soldier of Halpern, as well as the Anti-Modernizing Soldier so common in Latin America, are treated indiscriminately by our concept "pragmatic relevance of modernizing cleavages." We hypothesize only that such cleavages will cause military involvement, and do not argue which side the soldiers will take.

The Praetorian Soldier model of Huntington, which is akin to what Finer calls military-involvement-because-of-low-political-culture, is measured by our variable "strong civilian political institutions." Huntington's concept, unlike most of the others, has been adopted virtually without change: the only basic revision was to rework what he says about "institutionalization" so that tautology is explicitly avoided.

Finer's theories are considered to be a variation on the Praetorian Soldier Model, insofar as a "low political culture" (Finer's central concept) is really a way of saying that civilian political institutions are weak.

## OPERATIONALIZATION

Perhaps as unreliable as survey data, the aggregate data used to test these hypotheses could have been much harder. While more detailed data might have been gathered in a few countries or one region, (a) that would have made impossible any cross-regional generalizations, and (b) it would have made statistical analysis at the national level difficult, because of the dangerously large ratio of variables to cases. A number of interesting conclusions about differences between regions, as well as considerable stability in the statistical coefficients, resulted from our approach.

The 110 nation sample includes virtually all nations independent in the period under study. Specifically, the countries included are *all* the *sovereign* states—as defined by Russett, Singer, and Small (1968)—that were *independent* from Jan. 1, 1965 to Jan. 1, 1968, except:

(1) those that did not chose their own form of civil-military relations (this excludes the East European satellites of the Soviet Union, and Mongolia, which had their system imposed on them and maintained directly or indirectly by the Red Army);

(2) micro-states (Liechtenstein, Andorra, Vatican City, San Marino, Malta, Kuwait, the Maldive Islands, Singapore, and Western Samoa); and

(3) two units (Iceland and Mauritania) for which comparable data were, unfortunately, not readily available.

In analyzing these data, a low zero-order correlation coefficient was not deemed sufficient reason for exclusion of a variable from the model if it appeared likely that the independent variable might have a causal effect once other variables were controlled (partialled). Variables with a significant ($p < .10$) partial regression coefficient of proper sign were retained in the final causal model. The exact cut off for exclusion depended on the variable's importance in the theoretical literature as well as on the size of its coefficients.

Regressions were run using the entire variable set as predictors, and then using only the causal variables specified in the model. The beta coefficients reported in the findings are from the latter set of regressions. This is because the coefficients that were predicted to reduce to zero (prove spurious) did not always shrink exactly to zero. These unexplained deviations from the predicted indicate shortcomings either in theory or in data, and are thus valuable information. But they should not be included in the predictor equations, for they could introduce error effects into the estimation of the other coefficients, and thereby mask the effects of the causal variables measured.

Residuals were examined, and one region (Africa) was found to have very high positive and very high negative residuals. Clearly, the accepted explanations of military regime incorporated in the causal models were not accounting for African military involvement. The African cases were separated from the rest of the world in all future analyses, and the final coefficients reported are for the 80 non-African countries.

VARIABLE:  Relevance of Modernizing Cleavages

INDICATORS OF VARIABLE:  Urban-rural divisions
Literate-illiterate divisions

OPERATIONALIZATION:

Our first variable is the extent to which society is evenly divided into modern and non-modern groups. We operationalize this by assuming that literate groups and urban groups are relatively modernized, and illiterate groups and rural groups are relatively non-modernized. The two following graphs illustrate how the coding procedure was carried out. The percentage of literate population, and the percentage living in towns of more than 20,000 were plotted against military involvement. In both cases (see Graphs 3a and 3b) pyramidal graphs resulted: high levels of military involvement were associated with intermediate levels of urbanization and literacy; the levels of military involvement sloped down on either side to very low levels of M.I. for very developed and very underdeveloped literacy and urbanization levels. Both relationships were very strong for our data set, and differentiated sharply the military from the non-military countries. The highest category (10-20% urban and 35-45% rural) was assigned a one, then each category was assigned a number increasing with distance from the peak of the effect (see Graphs 4a and 4b). This transformation created a new line for both relationships (Graphs 5a and 5b). These (the last pair) were the lines estimated by the multivariate regression equation and reported in the findings.

There is one obvious inductive element in this procedure. It is assumed that 10-20% literate in cities greater than 20,000 and 35-45% of the adult population literate represents an even balance of forces between the modern and non-modern sectors. The only justification for using these specific percentages is the inductive rationale that they are the most strongly associated with military regimes.

The literacy data were taken from the following sources: Adelman and Morris (1967), percentage of adult population literate, approximately 1958; Banks (1970), percentage of population 17-64 literate about 1960; and U.N. *Compendia of Social Statistics* (1963; 1967), percentage of population 17-64 literate about 1960.

The data were coded into the following categories, which correspond to those of Adelman and Morris:

| Percentage Literate | Raw Score | Transformed Score |
|---|---|---|
| 0-6 | 1 | 1 |
| 6-11 | 2 | 3 |
| 11-16 | 3 | 5 |
| 16-23 | 4 | 7 |
| 23-30 | 5 | 9 |
| 30-35 | 6 | 11 |
| 35-45 | 7 | 12 |
| 45-55 | 8 | 10 |
| 55-65 | 9 | 8 |
| 65-75 | 10 | 6 |
| 75-85 | 11 | 4 |
| 85-100 | 12 | 2 |

[ 40 ]

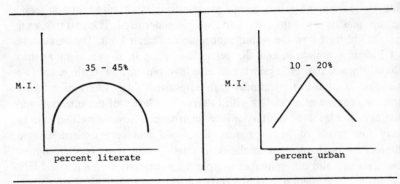

GRAPHS 3a and 3b: Military Involvement as a Function of Literacy Level and of Urbanization Level.

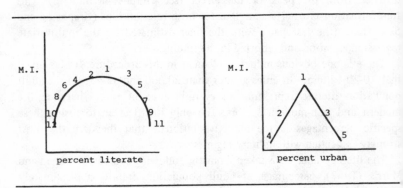

GRAPHS 4a and 4b: Military Involvement as a Function of Literacy Level and of Urbanization Level.

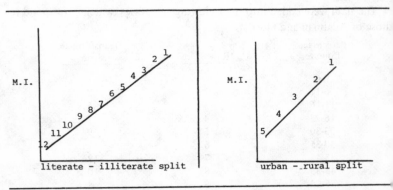

GRAPHS 5a and 5b: Military Involvement as a Function of Transformed Literacy and of Transformed Urbanization.

The urbanization data are from Adelman and Morris (1967: 25; percentage of population in urban areas of more than 20,000 inhabitants) and the U.N. *Compendia of Social Statistics* (percentage of population in cities of 20,000 or more, about 1960). The data were coded into the following categories:

| Percentage Urban | Raw Score | Transformed Score |
|---|---|---|
| 0-5 | 1 | 1 |
| 5-10 | 2 | 3 |
| 10-20 | 3 | 5 |
| 20-30 | 4 | 4 |
| 30-100 | 5 | 2 |

The next step was to convert the urbanization and literacy data into a single index of developmental conflicts. In the 110 cases the two measures correlated at r = 0.50. They were each converted into standardized scores and these scores were added together to get the index.

The index had a higher pair of correlations with the dependent variable than did either of its components:

CORRELATION MATRIX

| | M.I. 1960 | M.I. 1969 |
|---|---|---|
| Urban-rural split | −.32 | −.29 |
| Literate-illiterate split | −.42 | −.24 |
| Index of development cleavages | −.42 | −.31 |

VARIABLE: Discrimination and Potential Separatism

OPERATIONALIZATION:

Gurr's (1969) index of discrimination and potential separatism was used to measure this item. Briefly, the index measures the sum of (a) the percentage of the population discriminated against and (b) the percentage of the population with potentially separatist tendencies. As Gurr (1969: 121) says:

There appears to be no easy way to quantify for the purposes of cross-national comparison the *intensity* of deprivation associated with discrimination and separatism. We can, however, specify the proportion of the population which is potentially separatist or exposed to discrimination.

VARIABLE:   Urbanization Rate

INDICATOR OF VARIABLE:   Urbanization Rate in the 1950s

OPERATIONALIZATION:

Measuring a rate of change is a very difficult matter, since it requires comparable data from two appropriate points in time. Because of the difficulty involved in measuring urbanization rate when this study was begun, no one had calculated it for all the nations in the study. Now a somewhat similar indicator is available: Gurr's (1969: 53) index of decennial increase in migrants to cities.

Faced with the prospect of creating a new index, we proceded as follows. As the ideal indicator of rate of increase of urban population, we took the annual rate of increase in cities of over 100,000 population. This rate was usually calculated (using the formula below) from data in the U.N. *Compendia of Social Statistics* (1963; 1967).

We chose very large cities—those in which the population exceeded 100,000 at the start of the period—because Hypothesis 4 declares that rapid urbanization breeds fear and hostility by:

(1) creating major new groups (labor, middle class, industrialists) whose novelty in the political arena creates uncertainty as to their political behavior once in power,

(2) brings these groups together in a setting where conflicts between them are not mitigated by the cohesive forces of a small community, and where bad consequences (for example, unemployment) of these conflicts are not softened by the protection of community and extended family, and

(3) creates in these new groups a modern culture antithetical to the traditional culture, so that there exists two nations at the same time.

Implicit in each of these three mechanisms is an emphasis on the anonymity of city life, which creates fear and hostility because other groups which impinge on one's life are not well known or understood. Such anonymity should be greater the larger the city; hence urbanization was measured in cities of 100,000 rather than 20,000.

Outside of Africa, there were only a few countries with no cities of 100,000. In these few cases, annual increase of cities of 20,000 to 100,000 were used. In Africa, half the countries did not have cities over 100,000 during the full period, and data was extremely scarce for all countries. In the African cases, percentage of increase of capital city 1950-1967 (Morrison et al., 1972) was used.

To calculate the yearly rate of increase from data from two points in time, we used the formula $i = e^x - 100$, where $x = (\ln (f/p) - N)$, $i$ = rate of increase per year, $e = 2.178\ldots$, $p$ = the urban population at the first point in time, $f$ = the urban population at the second point in time, and $N$ = the number of years intervening. Thus, for example, if the population were initially 100,000 and increased to 506,000 over a 17 year period, the yearly rate of increase would be

$$\ln \left( \frac{506}{100} \right) = \ln 5.06$$

$$i = e^{[\ln (5.06)/17]} - 100 = 10\%$$

Data sources for urbanization rate include the U.N. *Compendia of Social Statistics,* Morrison et al. (1972), Hauser (1961), and Taylor and Hudson (1972).

VARIABLE: Divisiveness

OPERATIONALIZATION:

The operationalizations of urbanization rate and cleavage relevance—which interact to form divisiveness—have already been presented. Divisiveness was operationalized by multiplying these two variables together.

VARIABLES: External War
Domestic Violence

INDICATORS OF VARIABLE: External Wars, 1945-1968
Internal Wars, 1945-1968
Total Magnitude of Civil Violence,
1961-1963

OPERATIONALIZATION:

Wars were deemed to have psychological impact in proportion to the intensity of the wars fought, and in inverse proportion to the time elapsed between the present and the time the war occurred.

The total magnitude of civil violence 1961-1963 is an intensity measure assumed to be occurring contemporaneously with the periods of military involvement under study. The total magnitude of civil violence 1961-1963 is a complex index constructed by Gurr (1969) out of several highly intercorrelated items.

The intensity of the internal and external wars could have been measured in a number of ways, including the number of troops engaged, but was measured in terms of battle deaths because of available data.

The antiquity of the war was measured in terms of the years elapsed from its occurrence to the period of military involvement.

The impact of internal and external wars 1945-1968 was measured by multiplying the intensity of each war times how recently it occurred:

$$\text{IMPACT OF EACH WAR} = \text{INTENSITY} \times \left( \frac{\text{BEGINNING YEAR} + \text{FINAL YEAR}}{2} - 1945 \right)^2$$

Data for the intensity of the war, for its starting date and its concluding date, were gathered for all wars 1945-1968, as listed in the Stockholm International Peace Research Institute's *Yearbook of World Armament and Disarmament* (1970).

The intensity of a war was measured by the number of the battle casualties suffered in it. These casualties were scaled by the use of Richardson's scale (1960):

| Number of Deaths | Score Range |
|---|---|
| 31, 622, 777 to 3, 162, 278 | $7 \pm 1/2$ |
| 3, 162, 277 to 316, 228 | $6 \pm 1/2$ |
| 316, 227 to 31, 623 | $5 \pm 1/2$ |
| 31, 622 to 3, 163 | $4 \pm 1/2$ |
| 3, 162 to 317 | $3 \pm 1/2$ |
| 316 to 32 | $2 \pm 1/2$ |

It was assumed that the impact of wars declines with the passage of years. It was further assumed that their importance declined as a function of some constant times the square of the elapsed time: a war occurring in 1957 has a much greater—a hundred times greater by our algorithm—impact on 1968 than a war occurring in 1946. As one approaches the period of our study, a war in 1965 has four times the impact of a war in 1955.

We divided wars into three categories: coups, external wars, and internal wars. Coups were omitted to avoid tautology. "International wars" and "border conflicts" were treated as external wars—an exogenous variable in our model. Civil wars were treated as "internal wars"—an endogenous intervening variable in our model. Wars listed as both civil and international were divided 50-50 after scoring. For example, the Vietnam War 1962-1968 received a score of 6.0 for intensity, so its current impact score was:

$$\text{INTENSITY} \times \left( \frac{\text{END YEAR} + \text{STARTING YEAR}}{2} - 45 \right) = 6.0 \times 20^2 = 2400$$

Since the war seemed to us to be partially a civil war in South Vietnam, but an international war for North Vietnam, North Vietnam received 2400 points under external war, South Vietnam received 1200 points under external war and 1200 points under internal war. Obviously, this procedure is a bit subjective. It can be arbitrary, and even highly controversial in particular cases. However, the objective was not to pass moral judgment on particular cases, but rather to get some rough measures of the impact of a nation's involvement in external and internal wars.

A number of omissions existed in the Stockholm Institute's list. First, at least one major civil war—the bloody, decade-long racial war in the Sudan—was not included. We did not try to add any wars that they omitted. While no international wars have been omitted by the Institute, many instances of civil strife undoubtedly have been, so it is good to have Gurr's total magnitude of civil violence data in case the Internal War measure should fail us.

A second omission was that many wars were not given intensity scores. When this occurred, we assigned intensity scores as follows:

| Intensity | War |
| --- | --- |
| 6 | Vietnam War III (1962-1968), Nigeria-Biafra |
| 4 | Iraq-Kurds, Portugal-Mozambique, Cyprus 1967 |
| 2 | |
| 1 | all others (N = 30) |
| No hostilities | |

VARIABLE: Party System Strength

INDICATOR: Experts' Evaluations of Party System Strength

OPERATIONALIZATION:

The procedure we resorted to was to collect expert judgment on the degree of party system institutionalization. These judgments were extracted by examining the literature on party systems. Two books in particular proved useful because of their comparative tables: Huntington's *Political Order in Changing Societies* (1968) and Coleman's concluding analysis in the *Politics of the Developing Areas* (1960). Based on Huntington, the following scores on party system strength were assigned for the early 1960s:

## HUNTINGTON'S ROUGH RANKING OF
## PARTY SYSTEM STRENGTH

| Party System | Rank |
|---|---|
| Canada, U.K., Eire, Netherlands, Belgium, Luxembourg, Switzerland, Austria, Albania, Yugoslavia, U.S.S.R., Finland, Sweden, Norway, Denmark, C.P.R., North Korea, North Vietnam, Australia, New Zealand | 8 |
| Mexico, France, West Germany, Italy, Tunisia, Japan, India | 7 |
| U.S.A., Malaya | 6 |
| Jamaica, Venezuela, Peru, Chile, Uruguay, Guinea, South Korea, Ceylon | 5 |
| Argentina, Liberia, Tanzania | 4 |
| Brazil, Somalia, Philippines | 3 |
| Honduras, El Salvador, Nicaragua, Costa Rica, Panama, Colombia, Bolivia | 2 |
| Spain, Portugal | 1 |

Huntington does not tell us exactly what he means by "strength" in his "rough and impressionistic" ranking, but one must assume he is using the term as he had earlier defined it (1968: 12). Strength would then be a function of the scope of support and the level of institutionalization of the party system.

Coleman has a classification scheme in which he pegs one-party systems (in the peculiar terminology to be expected from Almond's pluralist ideology) on "overly participating" in government and politics. Dealing with African, Asian, and Latin American countries, Coleman produces the following classifications (1960: 562-567):

| Party system overly involved in Governmental Functions | Party system overly involved in Political Functions | Party system overly involved in both |
|---|---|---|
| South Africa | Cuba | Mexico |
| | Dominican Republic | Bolivia |
| | Honduras | Mali |
| | Paraguay | Ghana |
| | Tanganyika | Guinea |
| | Somalia | Ivory Coast |
| | Malawi | Central African Republic |
| | Algeria | Morocco |
| | Turkey | India |
| | Burma | Malaya |

When we examined those party systems that had been ranked by both Huntington and Coleman, we were struck by the high correlation of their rankings. Evidently, despite Coleman's ideological language, he ended up ranking the party systems more or less on how "strong" they were. As a result, his rankings could be merged with Huntington's. Countries classified as "over performing" one function tended to clump around three on Huntington's scale of strength, and party systems which over performed both sets of functions were clustered around seven. These numbers were assigned to the Coleman data, and then the two sets were merged into the following composite rank order:

| Party Systems (ca. 1960) | Composite Strength Coefficient |
|---|---|
| Canada, United Kingdom, Eire, Netherlands, Belgium, Luxembourg, Switzerland, Austria, Albania, Yugoslavia, U.S.S.R., Finland, Sweden, Norway, Denmark, C.P.R., N. Vietnam, N. Korea, Australia, New Zealand | 8 |
| France, West Germany, Italy, Japan | 7 |
| U.S.A., Mexico (6.5), Mali, Ivory Coast, Ghana, Central African Republic, Morocco, Tunisia (6.5), Israel, Taiwan, India (6.5), Malaya | 6 |
| Jamaica, Venezeula, Peru, Chile, Uruguay, Guinea (5.5), South Korea, Ceylon | 5 |
| Argentina | 4 |
| Cuba, Brazil, Paraguay, Tanzania (3.5), Somalia, Malawi, South Africa, Algeria, Turkey, Philippines | 3 |
| El Salvador, Nicaragua, Costa Rica, Panama, Colombia, Ecuador, Bolivia, Honduras (2.5), Libya (2.5) | 2 |
| Haiti, Dominican Republic, Guatemala, Spain, Portugal, Dahomey, Niger, Upper Volta, Sierra Leone, Togo, Cameroun, Nigeria, Gabon, Chad, Congo (Brazzaville), Congo (Kinshasha), Uganda, Kenya, Ruanda, Burundi, Ethiopia, Zambia, Malagasy, Libya, Sudan, Iran, Iraq, Egypt, Jordan, Saudi Arabia, Yemen, Afghanistan, Pakistan, Burma, Nepal, Thailand, Cambodia, South Vietnam, Indonesia | 1 |

VARIABLE: Modernization

INDICATOR OF VARIABLE: Harrison's (1970) Index of Modernization

OPERATIONALIZATION:

Harbison uses many indicators to create his index, which is based on the following variables:

(1) *per capita gross national product* at factor cost

(2) *per capita energy* consumption

(3) *newspaper* circulation per 1,000 population

(4) *radio* receivers per 1,000 population

(5) *telephones* per 1,000 population

(6) *motor vehicles* per 1,000 population

(7) *literacy rate* of adult population

(8) *doctors and dentists* per 10,000 population

(9) *nurses* per 10,000 population

(10) *hospital beds* per 10,000 population

(11) *daily animal protein* as proportion of total grams protein consumed

(12) *daily cereals and starches* as proportion of total calories consumed

(13) *life expectancy* at birth

(14) *first level* (5-14) educational enrollment

(15) *second level* (15-19) educational enrollment

(16) *third level* (20-24) educational enrollment

(17) first level *teachers* per 10,000 population

(18) second and third level *teachers* per 10,000 population

(19) per capita recurrent public *expenditures on education*

(20) percent of *population living in cities* of 20,000 and over

VARIABLE:  Government Financial Strength

INDICATOR:  Central Government Expenditures as a Percentage of Gross Domestic Product

OPERATIONALIZATION:

This indicator is taken from Gurr (1969: 102-120), who defends it as the best cross-national, available indicator of government financial strength.

To include the financial powers of state and local governments is, given the present state of social science data archives, an impractical task. This introduces some bias into the indicator, in that many federal states end up near the bottom of the list because their state government expenditures are not counted (of 117 nations, India, Switzerland and Mexico are 106th, 108th, and 112th, respectively); but this is a bias we must live with, for the indicator remains the best available and the cases of its bias are highly visible, as in the above three cases.

VARIABLE: Prior Levels of Military Rule

INDICATORS OF VARIABLE: Index of previous coups, 1900-1956
Level of Military Involvement in 1960
(when predicting level of military
involvement in 1969)

OPERATIONALIZATION:

To measure a nation's tradition of military involvement, one might proceed by the expert questionnaire technique used in assessing current levels of military involvement. But experts' memories as well as their data fade with the years, and the result would be great increases in unreliability as measurement moved back 20, then 30 or 40 years.

The frequency of military coups was deemed an inadequate measure of military involvement during a few years' period. This was primarily because their sporadic frequency is confusing in the short run:

(a) there are usually a few coups in the short run,

(b) their infrequent occurrence may indicate the stable position of a military regime that seized power just before the measurement period, and

(c) their frequent occurrence may indicate the demise of a previously strong military regime.

Over a 55 year period, however, temporary aberrations should cancel out, and over such a long period the number of coups should be a good indicator of military involvement.

Having thus decided to use coups as a measure of military tradition, we still had to decide the period in which to measure them. A good terminal year was 1956 because it was the last year prior to the 1957-1962 period in which the dependent variable was measured. Banks (1970) records each coup in each country, 1900-1965, and from this we could construct our list. We decided that 1900 was far enough back to ensure that traditional political forms before that would be either unimportant or should have made their impress on the 55 year period being measured.

Banks does not define coup but it apparently refers to *any* illegal, violent, domestically-caused change of regime. This introduces only a very slight bias, since in fact almost all the coups were military coups.

It seemed desirable to give more weight to two coups around 1950 than four coups back in the 1920s or eight coups in the period just before World War I. This was done by constructing the following index:

$$\text{COUP SCORE} = \sum_{i=1}^{N} \left( \begin{array}{c} \text{last two digits} \\ \text{of coup year} \end{array} \right)^2, \text{ where}$$

N = the number of coups the country suffered, 1900-1956.

For example, a country with eight coups in 1910 would receive a military tradition score of $8 \times (10)^2 = 800$. Another country with four coups in 1925 would receive a score of $4 \times (25)^2 = 2500$. A third country with two coups in 1950 would receive a score of $2 \times (50)^2 = 5000$.

VARIABLE:  Number of Years Independent

INDICATORS OF VARIABLE:  Just Independent
Years Independent

OPERATIONALIZATION:

Russett, Singer, and Small's (1968) list of twentieth century political units was used to count the number of years each nation was independent from 1900-1956. Maximum score was 56, minimum score zero. In the language of the authors of that list, "an entity was classed as *independent* if it enjoyed some measure of diplomatic recognition as well as effective control over its own foreign affairs and armed forces" (1968: 934).

This measure of years independent was used in testing Hypotheses 53 and 58. To test Hypothesis 11, we needed a measure sensitive to how recently the nation became independent. We did this by transforming the indicator "years independent" to the indicator "just independent" by recoding. Eight or more years independent was treated as the highest category (eight) of "just independent," and values one through seven on the scale were assigned for countries with one to seven years independence respectively.

VARIABLE:  Religon

INDICATORS OF VARIABLE:  Percentage of Population Moslem
or Catholic

OPERATIONALIZATION:

Nations were scored by the percentage of their population adhering to Islam or Catholicism. Data are from the first edition of the *World Handbook* (Russett et al., 1964). Baptismal records are the basis of the Catholic data. Informed estimates are the basis of the Moslem data, with an estimated error range of ± 10% (Russett et al., 1964: 248). We coded each nation on a scale of one to ten on the basis of what percentage of its population is Moslem or (exclusive) Catholic. Thus, if a nation is 82% or 87% Moslem or Catholic, it gets a score of nine.

> VARIABLE: Dominance of the Military Organization as a Fighting Force
>
> INDICATORS OF VARIABLE: Military participation ratios; internal security forces per 10,000 adults

OPERATIONALIZATION:

The military participation ratios from the *World Handbook II* were the measure used to test Hypothesis 3a. The assumption here is that the ratio of army, naval, and air force personnel (a rough equivalent of army personnel) to total population will be a good measure of the dominance of the military over other armed units.

To test Hypothesis 3b, the number of internal security forces was balanced against the number of military personnel. By internal security forces, Gurr (1969: 143) means what falls under our ordinary language terms "police," "gendarmerie," and "militia." Since in our data set the number of military personnel is always larger than the number of internal security forces, the ratio of one to the other is a good measure of the organized armed force strength available to the government in its effort to keep the regular military (army) in check.

Some missing data on internal security forces were filled in through the use of George Weeks' (1964) study.

## FINDINGS: A CAUSAL MODEL

The next step in our discussion will be a detailed account of the statistical analysis. We will state the criteria by which hypotheses were accepted as valid or rejected. We will report the beta coefficients that represent the strength of each causal arrow. The strong causal linkages will be assembled into a final, parsimonious causal model, and the amount of variance this model explains will be reported.

Elaborate multivariate testing which will be discussed below led to the elimination of a number of potential causal variables. The 10 that remained were included in the following causal models.

The causal models are parsimonious models based on the successive elimination of causal variables that did not contribute much to the percentage of variance explained. As a general rule, beta coefficients below /.10/ (that is, $-.10 < $ beta $ < .10$) were treated as evidence that no causal linkage existed between the two variables. This was done because:

(1) many coefficients were below /.10/, in contrast to the few above /.10/,

(2) the ones above /.10/ were always predicted by the theory,

(3) the ones below /.10/ were often unexpected and unpredicted, and it was difficult to explain their theoretical raison d'etre, and

(4) the ones below /.10/ often changed sign when minor changes were made in the countries included in the study or the variables entered in the stepwise regression.

If a variable's total effects on military involvement, when indirect effects were added to its direct effect, exceeded /.10/, the variable was retained. If a variable's effects exceed /.10/ in one regression (such as predicting the military involvement level in 1960) but not the other, the variable was retained in the model in both cases.

Some variables, such as military participation ratios (Hypotheses 4a and 4b) were dropped at the bivariate stage of analysis because their zero-order correlation coefficients were so small and their theoretical justification so weak that there seemed to be too great a chance they would contribute noise to the path analysis and too small a chance that the multivariate analysis would, by controlling for other variables, show them to have important direct and indirect effects.

Levels of statistical significance were not used to exclude variables because we are dealing with the whole population of contemporary regimes, and significance tests are intended to estimate confidence intervals for inferring population parameters when only sample statistics are available. Therefore, since a level of statistical significance had to be specified, a .10 level of statistical significance was used, since this level led to the exclusion of only a few variables whose beta weights were very near zero.

By these criteria, several variables proved to be of little importance in the path analysis. One must bear in mind that, while the strong relationships to be reported shortly are probably not the result of error, the weak relationships now discussed may be merely the result of measurement error, which can easily attenuate path (regression) coefficients.

The variables with very low coefficients include military participation ratios (Hypothesis 4a), military participation ratios as a percentage of internal security force ratios (Hypothesis 4b—MPR/ISF), and religion (Hypothesis 9).

M.P.R. and MPR/ISF are measured with a relatively high degree of accuracy, and so the evidence that they do not contribute much to military involvement must carry weight.

The statistics for these and all other variables are summarized in Table 3 which the reader should now scrutinize. These are the data used to construct the causal models discussed below.

The first causal model—presented in Figure 2—represents an attempt to explain military involvement in 1969 from causal variables measured around 1960. Nine variables account for 55% of the variance. The nine, in order of their causal effects on military involvement, are:

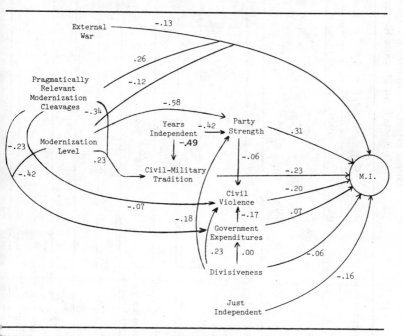

FIGURE 2: Path Diagram Showing Causal Effects on Military Involvement in 1960 (R$^2$ of nine variables = 58%)

TABLE 3
Direct Effects on Military Involvement:
Coefficients from Stepwise Regression

| Independent Variable | Beta 1969 | b 1969 | Simple r with M.I. 1969 | Simple r with M.I. 1960 | R² Increase 1969 | Number Variables Already Entered 1969 |
|---|---|---|---|---|---|---|
| Modernization Level | -.13 | -.01 | -.52 | -.49 | .27 | 0 |
| Party Strength | .34 | 2.40 | .51 | .53 | .09 | 1 |
| Relevance of Development Cleavage | .18 | .36 | .45 | .42 | .06 | 2 |
| Civil Violence | -.11 | -.43 | -.35 | -.40 | .025 | 3 |
| External War | -.15 | -.71 | -.10 | -.10 | .012 | 4 |
| Governmental Expenditures | .00 | .04 | .30 | .40 | .006 | 6 |
| Divisiveness | -.07 | -.24 | -.40 | -.38 | .006 | 7 |
| Hispanic | .10* | | -.25 | -.32 | | 10 |
| Religion | -.02** | | .25 | .30 | | 9 |
| Discrimination and Separatism | -.06+ | | .22+ | | | |

**TABLE 3 (Continued)**

| Coefficient Independent Variable | Beta 1969 | b 1969 | Simple r with M.I. 1960 | Simple r with M.I. 1969 | $R^2$ Increase 1969 | Number Variables Already Entered 1969 |
|---|---|---|---|---|---|---|
| Urbanization Rate | -.05+ | | | -.23+ | | |
| Internal War | .03* | | -.14 | -.07 | | |
| MPF | | | .07* | .03* | | |
| MPF/ISF | | | .16* | .17* | | |
| Civil-Military Tradition | | | -.46 | -.46 | | |
| Just Independent | | | -.14 | -.02 | | |
| Years Independent | | | -.07 | .03 | | |

*wrong sign; **not significant; +for 110 cases.

(1) Modernization level

(2) Party institutionalization

(3) Developmental cleavage, relevance of

(4) Civil-military tradition

(5) Rapid urbanization in a context of discrimination and potential separatism (divisiveness)

(6) External wars

(7) Total magnitude of violence

(8) Internal wars

(9) Central government expenditures as a percent of G.D.P.

The latter two variables contribute very little to the percentage of variance explained, and they have total effects of 0.03 and 0.02, respectively. Central government expenditure is reported only because it proves important in the causal model predicting military involvement in 1960. Internal war is reported because total magnitude of civil violence explains a large portion of variance and is tapping the same theoretical variable; this may depress the contribution of "internal wars."

When these two minor independent variables are dropped, the $R^2$ from the first seven is 53%. Adding the 1960 level of military involvement as an eighth predictor increases the $R^2$ to 66%.

The same variables were next used to predict military involvement in 1960. In this case the $R^2$ was 58% for nine variables and 56% for seven. The results are summarized in Figure 3.

One can compare (in Table 4) the total effects of the causal variables as they act in 1960 and then in 1969. More detailed breakdowns are provided in Tables 5 and 6. As can be seen in Table 4, with two exceptions the path coefficients are stable to within ± 0.07, and the two exceptions varied ± 0.09. The two major declines were in total magnitude of civil violence and in central government expenditures as a percent of the G.D.P. Possible reasons for the instabilities will be brought out as we discuss each variable in turn, but briefly, one reason for the two major declines may be that these variables were likely to fluctuate frequently over the 10 year interval, and expecting their level of one year to have a major causal effect exactly 10 years later may be inappropriate.

The reader may now wish to see in more detail how each causal variable contributed to these models. To show this, we will now present the findings for each hypothesis, beginning with the first. A summary of the direct effects hypotheses is provided in Table 7. Briefly, all hypotheses relating to legitimacy (L) were confirmed. The hypothesis (5) on political salience was confirmed. The hypotheses on cleavage intensity were all either confirmed or tentatively confirmed. The hypotheses on pragmatic relevance of cleavages were all confirmed or tentatively confirmed, except for the two involving the military participation ratios.

**Hypothesis 1**: *Modernization causes military involvement to decline. The direct effect of modernization was confirmed (beta .12 and .13).*

**Hypothesis 2**: *Governmental expenditures should reduce the level of military involvement. The hypothesized relationship was found to be very weak (beta .00 and .07).*

**Hypothesis 3a and 3b**: *Military participation ratios or the dominance of the military over internal security forces increase the level of military involvement. Both hypotheses were disconfirmed.*

**Hypothesis 4**: *Pragmatically relevant modernization cleavages cause military involvement. This hypothesis was confirmed. Direct effects betas were .18 and 26.*

**Hypothesis 5**: *Urbanization rate and discrimination interact to cause military involvement. This is based on the assumption that the intensity of cleavage and the relevance of cleavage interact to produce military*

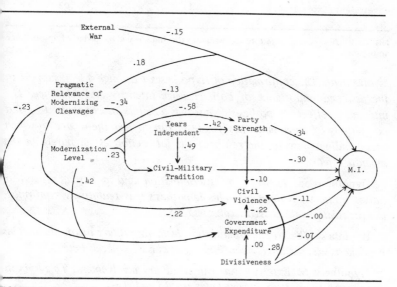

**FIGURE 3: Final Path Model Showing Causal Effects on Military Involvement in 1969 (R$^2$ of nine variables = 55%)**

**TABLE 4**
**Total Causal Effects of Each Variable**
**on Military Involvement**

| Variables, listed in order of importance of their effects | Total Effects on Military Involvement 1960 | Total Effects on Military Involvement 1969 |
|---|---|---|
| Modernization Level | -.40 | -.40 |
| Party Strength | .33 | .35 |
| Relevance of Modernizing Cleavages | .34 | .27 |
| Civil Violence | -.20 | |
| Military Tradition | -.18 | -.24 |
| Divisiveness | -.18 | -.17 |
| External Wars | -.13 | -.15 |
| Civil Violence | | -.11 |
| Government Expenditures | .11 | .02 |

NB: Civil Violence is listed twice because the data leave its order of importance ambiguous.

involvement. The confirmation of Hypotheses 1 through 4 lend support to the assumed importance of both cleavage intensity and relevance. The interaction effect—Hypothesis 5—also has a causal impact (beta .07). But no analysis of co-variance has yet been run to test the degree to which these findings may be the result of the interaction effect purely or the separate effects.

**Hypothesis 5a:** *Presence of discrimination and potential separatism causes military involvement. This hypothesis was tentatively confirmed, but the relationship proved weak: beta .05.*

**Hypothesis 5b:** *Rapid urbanization leads to military involvement. This hypothesis was tentatively confirmed, but at a weak level: beta .05.*

**Hypothesis 6:** *External wars cause military involvement. This hypothesis is confirmed: direct effects betas are .13 and .15.*

**TABLE 5**
**Direct and Indirect Effects on**
**Military Involvement, 1960**

| | | Magnitude of: | | |
|---|---|---|---|---|
| Causal Variables | Direct Effect | Indirect Effects, Listed by Intermediate Variable | | Total Effects |
| **Party System Strength** | .31 | **Civil Violence** | .01 | .32 |
| Level of Modernization | -.12 | Party Strength | -.18 | -.43 |
| | | Civil-Military Tradition | -.05 | |
| | | Govt. Expenditure | -.05 | |
| | | Civil Violence | -.03 | |
| | | | -.31 | |
| Relevance of Modernizing Cleavages | .26 | Civil-Military Tradition | .08 | .37 |
| | | Civil Violence | .01 | |
| | | Govt. Expenditure | .02 | |
| | | | .11 | |
| Military Intervention 1900-56 | -.23 | Party Strength | .05 | -.18 |
| Civil Violence | -.20 | | | -.20 |
| Divisiveness | -.06 | Civil Violence | -.05 | -.17 |
| | | Party Strength | -.06 | |
| | | Govt. Expenditure | .00 | |
| | | | -.11 | |
| External War | -.13 | | | -.13 |
| Central Government Expenditures of % of G.D.P. | .07 | Civil Violence | .04 | .11 |

**TABLE 6**
**Direct and Indirect Effects on**
**Military Involvement, 1969**

| | | Magnitude of: | | |
|---|---|---|---|---|
| Causal Variables | Direct Effect | Indirect Effects, Listed by Intermediate Variable | | Total Effects |
| Party System Strength | .34 | Civil Violence | .01 | .35 |
| Level of Modernization | -.13 | Party Strength | -.20 | -.42 |
| | | Civil-Military Tradition | -.07 | |
| | | Govt. Expenditure | .00 | |
| | | Civil Violence | -.02 | |
| | | | -.29 | |
| Relevance of Modernizing Cleavages | .18 | Civil-Military Tradition | .09 | .28 |
| | | Civil Violence | .01 | |
| | | Govt. Expenditure | .00 | |
| | | | .10 | |
| Military Intervention 1900-56 | -.30 | Party Strength | .06 | -.24 |
| Civil Violence | -.11 | | | -.11 |
| Divisiveness | -.072 | Civil Violence | -.03 | -.17 |
| | | Party Strength | -.0749 | |
| | | Govt. Expenditure | .00 | |
| External War | -.15 | | | -.15 |
| Central Government Expenditures as % of G.D.P. | .00 | Civil Violence | .02 | .02 |

**TABLE 7**

| CONCEPT | DERIVED HYPOTHESES | CONFIRMED OR DISCONFIRMED |
|---|---|---|
| S | H.1: level of modernization | C |
| | H.2: low governmental expenditures | C |
| | H.3a: MPR | D |
| | H.3b: MPP/ISF | D |
| S-Z | H.4: relevant modernizing cleavages | C |
| Z | H.5b: urbanization rate | TC |
| X | H.5a: discrimination and potential separatism | TC |
| | H.7: civil violence | C |
| X(S-Z) | H.5: urbanization rate times discrimination and separatism | C |
| L | H.7: civil violence | C |
| | H.6: external wars | C |
| | H.8: political parties' strength | C |
| | H.9: religious authoritarianism | D |
| | H.10: previous military rule | C |
| CONTROL | H.11: recent independence | C |

C = confirmed; TC = tentatively confirmed; D = disconfirmed

**Hypothesis 7**: *Domestic violence causes military involvement. This hypothesis is considered confirmed because of the strong impact of total magnitude of civil violence (beta .11 and .20).*

**Hypothesis 8**: *Political parties' strength causes low levels of military involvement. The hypothesis was confirmed, and the effect was found to be very strong (betas .31 and .34).*

**Hypothesis 9**: *Authoritarian religions (Catholicism and Islam) cause military involvement. This hypothesis was disconfirmed (beta −.02—not significant).*

**Hypothesis 10**: *Previous military rule causes military involvement. As mentioned above, autocorrelation and time-lag causation make it difficult to test this hypothesis and its subsidiaries (cultural tradition of military rule and regime continuity). Nevertheless, it is encouraging that civil-military tradition 1900-1956 and level of military involvement 1957-1962 are related to military involvement 1969 (beta .17 and .55 respectively, and together they account for a 0.20 increase in $R^2$ even though they are forced into stepwise regression at the last step).*

**Hypothesis 11**: *Very recent independence decreases the level of military involvement. This hypothesis was confirmed (beta .16).*

**Hypothesis 12**: *Modernization causes party institutionalization. The effects here were confirmed and found to be strong (beta .58). The indirect effects of modernization, working through party system strength, on the level of military involvement were high (−.18 and −.20).*

**Hypothesis 13**: *Divisiveness weakens party institutionalization. The predicted relationship did occur (beta −.22). The indirect effects of divisiveness on military involvement were −.06 and −.075 along this path.*

**Hypothesis 14**: *The longer since independence, the greater the party institutionalization. This relationship was strong in the wrong direction (beta −.42). Other things (level of modernization, divisiveness, military involvement tradition) being equal, it appears that a recent struggle for national independence strengthens the party system.*

**Hypothesis 15**: *With a time lag, military involvement probably weakens party institutionalization. The biggest surprise in the study was the disconfirmation of this hypothesis. The betas between military involvement tradition and current party system strength are in the wrong direction (.17). The indirect effects of past military involvement on current military involvement are .05 and .06. This may indicate that Huntington is correct in asserting that party institutionalization affects* military involvement and not vice versa. One possible explanation of the positive coefficient between past military involvement and present party system strength is that nations have tended to go through stages of political development, and that a stage in which political parties flourish follows the stage in which military involvement is most likely.

**Hypothesis 17**: *Modern nations will have a low level of traditional military involvement. This hypothesis was confirmed (beta .23). By this intervening variable, modernization had an indirect effect on contemporary military involvement (−.05 and −.07).*

**Hypothesis 18**: *The more pragmatically relevant the modernizing cleavages, the higher the level of traditional military involvement. This hypothesis was confirmed (beta −.34). The indirect effect on contemporary military involvement was strong (.08 and .09).*

**Hypothesis 19**: *The longer the period of independence the greater the opportunity for a military involvement tradition to have developed. This hypothesis was confirmed (beta .47).*

**Hypothesis 21**: *Divisiveness increases the total magnitude of civil violence. This hypothesis was confirmed (beta −.23). The indirect effect on military involvement was weak (−.05 and −.03).*

**Hypothesis 22**: *The higher the central government expenditures, the lower the total magnitude of civil violence. This hypothesis was of course confirmed (beta −.17), since Gurr found the same relationship with the same data. Indirect effects on military involvement were very weak (.02 and .04), but again in the predicted direction.*

**Hypothesis 23**: *Party system strength decreases the total magnitude of civil violence. A weak (beta −.06) relationship exists, but the indirect effects on military involvement (.01 and .01) are trivial.*

**Hypothesis 24**: *Pragmatic relevance of development cleavages increase the total magnitude of civil violence. This hypothesis was weakly confirmed (beta −.07). The indirect effects on military involvement were virtually nil (.01).*

**Hypothesis 25**: *The higher the level of modernization, the lower the total magnitude of civil violence. This hypothesis was confirmed (beta −.17), but the indirect effects on military involvement were small (−.02 and −.03).*

**Hypothesis 27**: *The more modern, the higher the central government expenditures as a percentage of gross domestic product. The hypothesis was confirmed, and at a strong level (beta −.42). The indirect effects on* *military involvement were small (−.05 and .00), however, because of the weak effects of central government expenditures on military involvement.*

**Hypothesis 28**: *The greater the pragmatic relevance of cleavages, the lower the level of central government expenditures. This hypothesis was also confirmed at a moderately strong level (beta −.23), but again the indirect effects were weak for the same reasons.*

**Hypothesis 29**: *The more salient the cleavages, the lower the level of central government expenditure. This hypothesis was not confirmed (beta .00).*

This completes the reporting of the results on indirect effects. Figure 4 presents a final, parsimonious model of the findings.

## CONCLUSIONS

What are the implications of these results for the leading theories of military rule? Having briefly summarized our set of hypotheses, we will now review how the theories of the Garrison State, the Praetorian Soldier, the Modernizing Soldier, the Professional Soldier, and Andreski are related to our model; we will accompany this review of the major theories with a description of how they fared in the empirical testing.

In discussing Andreski, we must point out that many of his concepts, especially his concept of social "homogeneity," are too vague for comparison with the variables in our model. A portion of our model shows that divisiveness and relevance of cleavages cause civil war, which in turn causes military involvement. This portion of the model is an intellectual descendent of Andreski's argument that heterogeneity and poverty cause violence, which in turn cause military involvement. In general, our testing revealed these indirect effects to be weak but in the predicted direction.

Andreski's proposition that the size of the army affects the level of military involvement has, of course, a much more direct analog in our hypotheses about M.P.R. and MPR/ISF ratios. These two hypotheses were both disconfirmed.

Lasswell's Garrison State model is embraced by our hypothesis on the effects of external war. This hypothesis was confirmed. But several other variables proved more important or just as important as external war in affecting the level of military involvement. It is because of the confounding effects of these other variables that external wars have not produced military rule in *developed* countries, as Lasswell had predicted.

The Modernizing Soldier of Halpern and the *Anti*-Modernizing Soldier so common in Latin America are treated indiscriminately by our concept

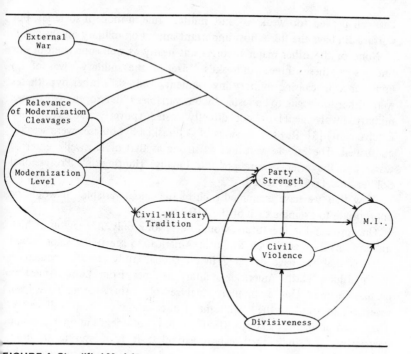

**FIGURE 4: Simplified Model**

"pragmatic relevance of modernizing cleavages." We hypothesize only that such cleavages will cause military involvement, and do not argue which side the soldiers will be on. The important causal impact of such cleavages on military involvement is strongly confirmed by our statistical analysis. Both in terms of its direct and its indirect effects, this variable proves to be the second and third most important in our model.

The Praetorian Soldier model of Huntington, which is akin to what Finer calls military-involvement-because-of-low-political-culture, is measured by our variable "strong political party system." The importance of this variable appears to be very great. In terms of its direct effects, it is the most important causal variable. Only modernization is more important in its total effect on military involvement.

Finally, the Professional Soldier model of Huntington seemed too discredited to merit testing, given the high costs of gathering data.

In short, of the major theories in the field, the Praetorian model of Huntington (and Finer) fared best. The Modernizing Soldier was not directly tested, but modernizing conflicts on which the military could take either side were second in importance. The Garrison State model of

Lasswell proved too weak to cause military rule in modern societies, but warfare did have the third most important impact on military involvement.

None of the other major theories was nearly as well supported in our findings as these three. Andreski's "size of the military" was of no importance in causing military involvement. Andreski's other hypotheses were either too vague to be tested by our variables ("heterogeneity" causes military involvement) or not directly tested (poverty causes military involvement).[3] Revised versions of Andreski's hypotheses were weakly confirmed. The effects were not as strong as that of Lasswell's external wars, but the effects were present. Finally, Huntington's Professional Soldier model was not tested.

Now that we have examined each of the causal variables, it would be appropriate to examine each of the 110 cases.

One project for the future would be to look only at a region of high military involvement, such as Latin America, to see if the same causal patterns that we have detected in our global study are also evident in distinguishing Latin American military regimes from Latin American civilian regimes. Our preliminary analyses of Latin America have been severely hampered by the small number of cases and by multi-collinearity. These two problems make it difficult to have confidence in the regression coefficients for individuals causal variables. It is reassuring to note, however, that six of our causal variables explain 55% of the variance in the Latin American cases. The six variables are, in declining order of importance, the party system strength, the prior tradition of military rule (1900-1956), the pragmatic relevance of developmental cleavages, the total magnitude of civil violence, the number of years since independence, and the central government expenditures as a percentage of gross domestic product.

Examining the residuals, the African cases leap to our attention. They are almost all poorly predicted: huge positive and negative residuals abound. The model explains only 10% of the variance for the African cases. This is why the African cases were dropped before doing all the causal models: the African cases are responding to different causal patterns, and to include them only makes the analysis murky.

Why did the African cases differ so sharply from the rest of the world? An attempt must be made to explain this. After all, how useful is a theory that cannot account for its own inapplicability to almost 30% of the cases studied?

Two things that may distinguish African regimes are (1) that they are newly formed regimes in territories that usually have no reason for being communities other than their shared former colonial status, and hence (2 that their political systems may respond less to the rest of the social system (which contains most of our causal variables, and with which the African political systems are unintegrated) than it does to such outside disturbances as the character of military and civilian leaders and the activities of foreign powers.

This general line of thought may be operationalized as follows.

*General African Hypothesis:* In Africa, politics is not yet as institutionalized, interrelated a part of the general domestic social system as it is elsewhere. From this general hypothesis the following hypotheses follow:

*Corollary A:* African military involvement is more likely to be influenced by external than by domestic events.

*Corollary B:* The number of months since the mother country granted independence will be proportional to the intensity of military involvement.

*Corollary C:* The intervention of troops from the mother country to prevent a coup will reduce the level of military involvement.

*Corollary D:* The occurrence of coups in neighboring countries is a cause of military involvement.

*Corollary E:* Social characteristics, such as total magnitude of civil violence, cleavages, divisiveness, and central government expenditures as a percentage of gross domestic product, are weakly related to military involvement in Africa.

*Corollary F:* Personal characteristics of individual political and military leaders and of groups of military officers will have a strong influence on African military rule.

## SUMMARY

Although there were imperfect linkages between our variables and measurement, and although the confirmed hypotheses were not perfectly integrated into the theoretical decision-making structure, a number of tentative conclusions can be drawn from the theory and supporting data.

Our theory, which received some support from the data, emphasized that military involvement is determined by the *balance* between L, the value attached to civilian *institutions, and* $(S-Z)X$, a set of terms measuring the salience of *cleavages* between groups in the political system. Military involvement in politics *cannot* be explained *only* in terms of the strength of central political *institutions* (as Huntington's Praetorian theory tends to do) or only in terms of social *cleavages* (as Andreski, Halpern, Johnson, and Lieuwen tend to do). In the pure legitimacy of institutions' point of view, military involvement seems a sign of childishness and immaturity—"if only they would learn to respect common norms for resolving differences!" But in the cleavage view, the cohesive power of loyalties to common institutions tends to get overlooked. Military involvement is more appropriately viewed as controlled by a *balance* of values, in which increases in the scope and intensity of X, the stakes of political conflict, must be matched by increases in L, the loyalty to civilian institutions, if military involvement is to remain at the same level.

Huntington argues that military rule is one consequence of an imbalance between the level of political institutionalization and the level of social mobilization. Thus, Huntington argues that if social mobilization increases and political institutionalization does not, military rule becomes more likely.

Huntington, in our view, is misleading: social mobilization per se does not increase the level of military involvement. The *rate* of social mobilization increases the level of military involvement only if the cleavages and conflicts between the newly mobilized groups remain salient. Military rule is the consequence of an imbalance between level of political institutionalization (L) and the salience of political cleavages $[(s-z)x]$.

In contrast to Huntington, we argue that the level of social mobilization, *ceteris paribus, decreases* the level of military involvement in politics. It does so by making it difficult for the military to control the large number of civilians who, when the level of mobilization is high, are aware of their government, have preferences about its activities, and want to have the kind of say over what it should do that they cannot exercise under military rule.

In the light of these findings, it may no longer be appropriate to interpret military rule as one aspect of "political disorder." Our explanation of military rule begins to look very different from the explanation of student riots, revolutionary turmoil, the total magnitude of civil violence and other aspects of "political disorder."

Hence, although variables related to Huntington's theory of Praetorianism were the most important predictors of the level of military involvement, it would be wrong to conclude that Huntington's theory is fully compatible with our argument. Huntington puts too much emphasis on legitimacy (L), and implies that it is merely the expansion of participation and social mobilization that presents a challenge to civilian institutions, whereas we have emphasized that it is the salience of cleavages that puts strains on civilian government. This is the difference between visions of a milling mob and visions of a rational coalition dedicated to insuring the preservation or achievement of a way of life that its members value. It is the difference between seeing the use of force as "disorder" and seeing it as the rational pursuit of goals in an environment involving irreconcilable differences. Amongst other things, the latter view, which we have adopted, carries with it more precise predictions of the timing of military involvement.

The formula we have employed, $L < (s-z)x$, allows us to emphasize how other writers have been over-zealous in pushing preeminence of one or the other side of the inequality: Huntington overemphasizes the L, and the conflict theorists stress the other side of the inequality.

The inequality is also useful because it allows us to relate ideas that once stood alone, such as those of Lasswell on the Garrison State, to the ideas of the other writers. For example, in the inequality, Lasswell's ideas fall under the category L—the relative legitimacy of civilian and military rule. Andreski's emphasis on the military participation ratio (M.P.R.) is also something we can incorporate into our organizing scheme. We took his emphasis on the military participation ratio to be an emphasis on the role of brute force in affecting the potential success (S) of military involvement. Insofar as brute force affected the potential success of military involvement, the military participation ratio should affect the level of military involvement. Since the statistical analysis indicated that M.P.R. was unrelated to military involvement, we concluded that brute force was not a very effective form of power in civil-military relations. Hence, we were able to conclude that the element S was affected more by the level of political mobilization of civilians than by the brute strength of the military as measured by the proportion of men in the army.

In brief, our theory provided a general framework within which to integrate the writings of several theorists on military involvement, and our empirical testing allowed us to check loosely the validity of the theory and to state more concretely what are and what are not important features of legitimacy (L), cleavage intensity (X), and cleavage relevance (s−z), the three components of the decision rule which we derived from the assumptions of our theory.

## NOTES

1. For a synopsis of the literature, see Amos Perlmutter's (1970) overview. The terms Praetorian Soldier, Modernizing Soldier, and Garrison Soldier are Perlmutter's.

2. Proposition 2b here called into question by the "urban villager" phenomenon, but even if proposition 2b is false the other assertions should suffice to validate the argument.

3. Our data do show that *modern* countries are less violent and less dominated by the military than non-modern ones, even when other variables are controlled for; it could be argued that this is good evidence for Andreski's proposition about poverty.

## REFERENCES

ADELMAN, I. and C. T. MORRIS (1967) Society, Politics, and Economic Development. Baltimore: Johns Hopkins Univ. Press.

ALMOND, G. and J. COLEMAN [eds.] (1960) The Politics of the Developing Areas. Princeton: Princeton Univ. Press.

ANDERSON, C. (1967) Politics and Economic Change in Latin America. New York: Van Nostrand Reinhold.

ANDRESKI, S. (1968) Military Organization and Society. Berkeley: Univ. of California Press.

BANKS, A. (1970) Cross Polity Time Series Data. Cambridge: M.I.T. Press.

DEUTSCH, K. (1961) "Social mobilization and political development." Amer. Polit. Sci. Rev. 55 (September): 493-502.

FINER, S. E. (1971) Comparative Politics. New York: Basic Books.

——— (1962) The Man on Horseback. New York: Praeger.

FLERON, F. (1969) "Towards a reconceptualization of political change in Soviet Union." Comparative Politics 1 (January): 228-244.

GURR, T. with C. RUTTENBERG (1969) Cross National Studies of Civil Violence. Washington, D.C.: Amer. Univ. Center for Research in Social Systems.

HALPERN, M. (1963) The Politics of Social Change in the Middle East and North Africa. Princeton: Princeton Univ. Press.

HARBISON, F., J. MARUHNIC, and J. RESNICK (1970) Quantitative Analyses of Modernization and Development. Princeton: Industrial Relations Section, Princeton Univ.

HAUSER, P. [ed.] (1961) Urbanization in Latin America. New York: International Documents Service.

HEISE, D. (1969) "Problems in path analysis and causal inference," pp. 38-73 in E. Borgatta [ed.] Sociological Methodology, 1969. San Francisco: Jossey Bass.

HUNTINGTON, S. (1968) Political Order in Changing Societies. New Haven: Yale Univ. Press.

——— (1957) The Soldier and the State. Cambridge: Harvard Univ. Press.

JOHNSON, J. [ed.] (1962) Role of the Military in the Underdeveloped Countries. Princeton: Princeton Univ. Press.

KLING, M. (1956) "Towards a theory of power and political instability in Latin America." Western Polit. Q. 9 (March): 21-35.